UNQUALIFIED.
UNWORTHY.
Still Chosen.

GOD CHOSE ME ANYWAY.

BY TE-ERRA DAVIS

Foreword by Kai Fleming
Proofreading: Haley G
Interior Design & Typesetting: TeaBerryStudio.com
Cover Design: KMS Arafat
Marketing & Brand Support: Fleming Marketing Consultant

Published by Renewed Ink
Baltimore, Maryland

Printed by Ingram Spark & Lulu Direct

ISBNs:
Paperback: 979-8-9940877-0-1
Hardcover: 979-8-9940877-1-8
eBook: 979-8-9940877-2-5
Audiobook: 979-8-9940877-3-2

First Edition
Printed in the United States of America

For speaking requests, permissions, or inquiries:
tdavis@renewedink.com

www.renewedink.com

DEDICATION

To my Lord and Savior, Jesus Christ —
This book would not exist if You hadn't given me the vision and the direction to write it.
Thank You for trusting me with this assignment. For carrying me when I was too weak to stand. For never letting go, even when I tried to run. I am forever grateful for Your grace, Your mercy, and Your unshakable love. May every word on these pages reflect Your heart and point people back to You.

To my children —
You are my greatest earthly gifts.
Each of you gave me a reason to fight, to pray, and to keep going.
You've seen me at my lowest and loved me anyway.

This book is part of our story too — a testimony that God redeems, restores, and still has a plan.

To the ones who feel lost —
This is for you.
For the ones who think they've gone too far…
That they've messed up too much…
That God won't take them back because they'll just disappoint Him again.

Please hear me: He still wants you.
He's still calling you.
You are not too late.
You can always come home.

CONTENTS

FOREWORD

As Christians, especially when we come to the faith, many think things will become easy once we come to Christ, and storms will no longer hit. That is far from true. The word clearly says in Isaiah 54:17, "no weapon formed against you shall prosper, and every tongue which rises against you in judgment you shall condemn. This is the heritage of the servants of the LORD, and their righteousness is from Me," Says the Lord." The word demonstrates that storms will come, but they do not have the power to prevail over you.

Te-erra and I first met in 2023 in VA while I was in graduate school, and during that time, I was actually in a storm. We met through a Discord chat centered on Christ. One day, she dropped a message about an abstinent Christian group called TST, and I jumped on it quickly. I was starting the journey of becoming abstinent and trying to figure out my walk with Christ at the moment, and I needed community. I didn't know our friendship would develop into what it did today. Looking

back, I see her age, two different upbringings, and two completely different walks of life, but what united us was her heart
to serve others and to pursue a relationship with Christ. I don't
thank her enough, but her heart for serving and being there
for others is one of the main reasons I am writing this today.
Her checking in on me, even when I was silent in my storms,
and Te-erra had no idea, was what I needed to keep moving
forward. I am thankful for her obedience and for God sending
such a genuine heart to me in my time of need. Throughout
the years, I can say that she has demonstrated and continues
to show what it means to be the hands and feet of Jesus. The
genuine heart you see is what you will get at all times. Te-erra
is a uniter, a powerful voice, a leader, and a caring mother, but
I am glad to call her my friend.

Her new book, Unqualified. Unworthy. Still Chosen is not a marriage book, not a trauma, shame, disappointment book, but it is
a book about how God left the 99 to find you. Those other top-
ics are just branches of the tree, but the foundation is grounded
on the Lord finding you in your mess. God did not call you to
shower before you come to him, but He called you to go to him
dirty so he can wash you clean with His blood from all sin. This
book will feel like a rollercoaster because many of you can relate
to this story but have been silent about it. This book may be the
nudge to face your mess head-on, but not alone, with the Lord.
Te-erra has dealt with divorce, motherhood struggles, abuse,
self-doubt, shame, and the list goes on, but the woman you see
today, who beat all the odds, is not the same woman that you will
be reading in this book. The vulnerability is powerful because

many people only show the finished product, never explaining the journey that got them there. You get all of that and then some. With this book, it may be a testimony, but Te-erra never fails to help whoever she can with resources, application questions, and scripture.

I highly recommend that everyone read this book because it will press buttons that will hurt. This book is not a feel-good book, but one meant to wring out all the shame and disappointment within you and to call you to surrender fully at God's throne. When you think of Peter on the boat in the storm with the other disciples in Matthew 14:22-33, Peter could walk on water because he kept his eyes on what mattered: Jesus. However, when he took his eyes off Jesus, he began to drown because his eyes were too focused on the chaos around him. Many of us have had moments when we are like Peter, prevailing, and then begin to drown and wonder how we got there. We all have been guilty. This book calls us all to keep our eyes on Jesus because when we lock our eyes on Him, peace surrounds our whole being, our minds are clear, and we are free. God has assigned Te-erra to write this book as a resource to point back to the source, the word. I know this book will impact many people. Buckle up and prepare for a ride. The road may be bumpy, but you will get to the destination, whole and new!

Your Brother in Christ,
Kai Fleming

PREFACE

This book was not born out of ambition. It was born out of obedience. I never planned on telling these stories — especially not the ones that exposed the worst parts of my own character. But God gave me the vision, and I couldn't shake it. This wasn't just a good idea. It was a divine assignment. I wrote this book because I know what it feels like to be drowning in shame, buried under grief, and haunted by decisions that can't be undone. I know what it's like to believe God has moved on without you. I also know what it's like to realize afterward… He never did.

Throughout every storm I waded, through the abuse and the betrayal, the poverty and the single motherhood — the spiritual silence — God was writing something bigger than just my pain. He was writing redemption. And not just for me, but for anyone else whose story might feel too stained for grace. This book is for the broken, the tired, and the angry. The ones who have given up but still always felt that quiet pull to return home.

There is no perfect structure here. No one-size-fits-all formula. Just truth. Just my heart. Just my real, raw testimony stitched together with the thread of God's unrelenting love. I have made peace with the fact that this book won't be for everyone — but it will be for someone.

And that someone might be you.

So, before you turn the page, just know this: God is still in the business of rescuing people. And if you're reading this, it means He hasn't given up on you.

He never will.

INTRODUCTION

"I Wasn't Supposed to Write This Book"

Let me be honest. I didn't want to write this.
Truthfully, I didn't think I had any right to.

Why would anyone listen to me?

I've been abused, and I've done damage too.
I've cheated. I've lied. I've lost control.
I've stayed in relationships that were slowly destroying me.
I've questioned God. Yelled at Him. Ignored Him. And wondered if He was even real.

There were seasons where I looked at my life and thought:
"There's no way God still wants me."

But somehow… He did.
Not because I had it all figured out.
Not because I cleaned myself up.
But because God wouldn't let me stay lost.

This book is not for people who have it all together.
It is not for those who always say the right thing or know all the scriptures.

This is for the one who feels dirty. Unseen. Angry. Ashamed. The one who feels like they've gone too far, messed up too much, or stayed stuck too long.

I wrote this for the person who continues to choose survival over healing.
For the one who prays but still feels numb.
For the one who sits in church every week but silently wonders if any of it is real.

For the one who keeps smiling in public while falling apart in private.
For the one who left—and got judged.
And for the one who stayed—and lost themselves.

I want you to know something I wish someone told me earlier:
God still sees you.
God still wants you.
God still calls you.

You don't have to perform and you don't have to pretend.
This book isn't a "how to fix your life" manual.
It's not a sermon.
It's a story.
My story.

Of what happens when God finds you in your mess—and chooses you anyway.

Because He doesn't choose the obvious.
He chooses the overlooked.

If you're tired of the front, tired of religion, tired of feeling like you'll never be "good enough" for God—this is for you.
If you're still in a mess but hoping for more—keep reading.
We're going there. For real.
Together.

Part One

WHEN EVERYTHING FELL APART

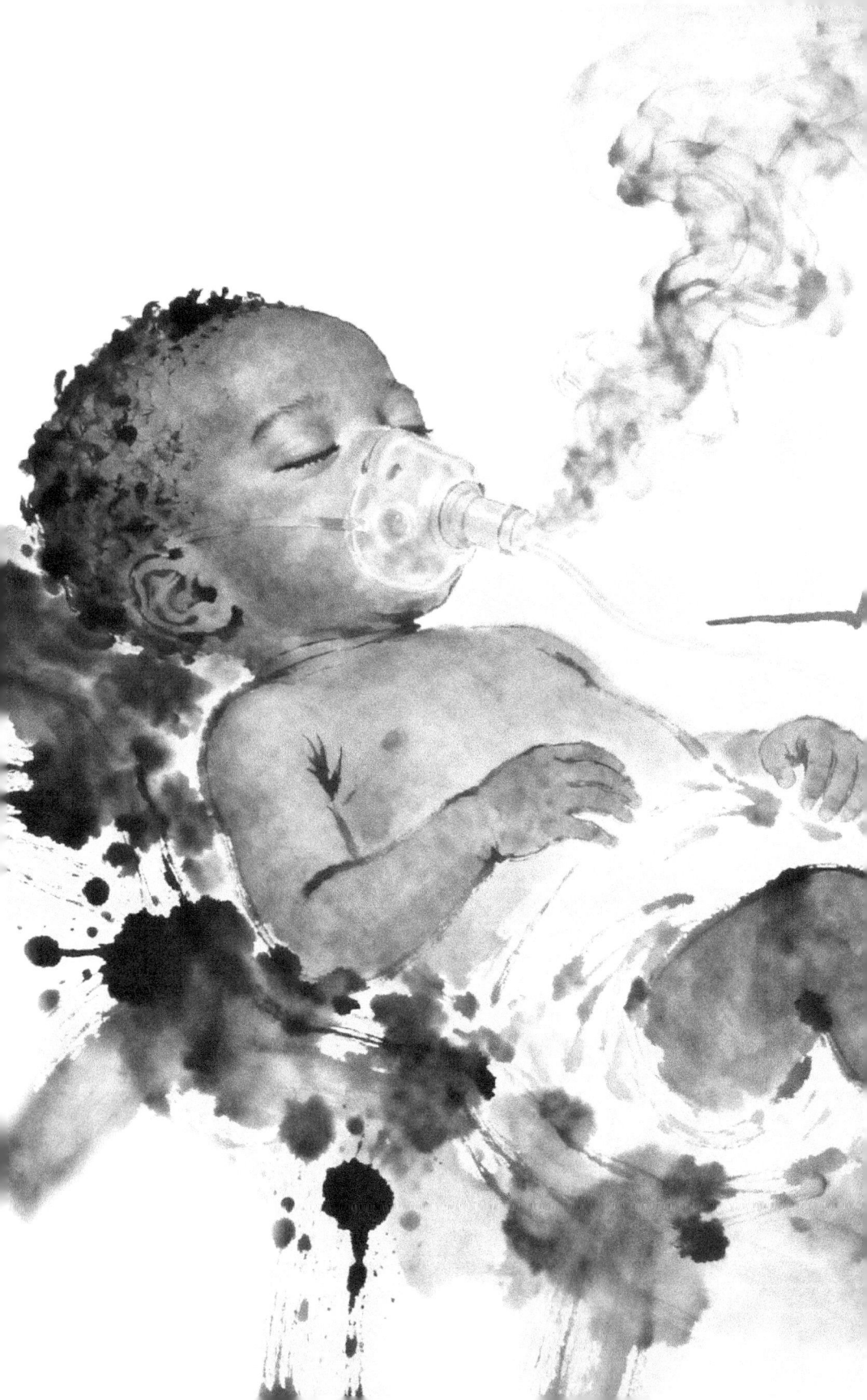

MY BABY COULDN'T BREATHE, AND I COULDN'T PRAY

NICU Nights, Medical Battles, and a Fragile Faith

My son was born at 23 weeks and 6 days. A micro-preemie. Nothing could have prepared me for what happened next. The doctors told me he wasn't breathing, and then asked me a question no mother ever expects to hear: Do you want to pull the plug?

I looked at my son's father and told him, "You better go talk to her before I do." We were all in the delivery room praying, crying, and covering my son with desperate hope. Finally, the nurse said, "We got him to breathe."

A sigh of relief fell over the room. But before I could even process what had just happened, they were rushing him out. I hadn't seen his face. I hadn't heard his cry. I told his father to go and follow him, because I didn't even know what my son looked like.

They didn't bring him to me. They just took him away.

And I couldn't go after him because I wasn't done either. I had to undergo emergency surgery, as some of the placenta had remained inside me. They said if it wasn't removed, I could have died.

It is crazy how much God has covered me in my life. I could have died. My son could have died. But He kept me, and He kept us.

Later that night, after the epidural wore off, I made my way to the NICU. There he was. 1 pound and 15 ounces inside a plastic box, hooked up to what felt like every machine in the room. I couldn't control myself. A yell escaped me. A deep, painful cry that echoed from somewhere I didn't even know existed. I backed away out of the room, and cried all the way back to mine.

That night, I wrote out Jeremiah 29:11 on a piece of paper: "For I know the plans I have for you, declares the Lord…"

I taped it to his incubator that night and then ran right back out. I couldn't stay. Seeing him like that shattered me. At the door, a nurse stopped me and asked if I was okay. I wasn't, but I nodded. Then she asked if she could pray with me.

Of course she could.

The next few days were a blur of tears and silence. I cried when I had to leave the hospital without him. Who really leaves the hospital without their baby? That's not how things were supposed to go. It felt like my heart was still in the NICU while my body was walking out the door.

He stayed there for five months.

During that time, he underwent multiple surgeries. Brain surgery, GI surgery, and hernia repairs. I was a brand-new mom navigating feeding tubes, oxygen monitors, medical jargon, and silent nights filled with worry. I didn't know what to expect when he came home. We had so many specialty doctors, outpatient appointments, and ER visits that for the first three or four years of his life, it felt like I spent most of my time in hospital rooms. Either prepping for surgery or recovering from it.

And watching your child suffer? That's a pain I wouldn't wish on my worst enemy. When your child can't eat before a surgery, but cries out for food that you can't give him, or when they wake up in pain and all you can do is hold them. That is an ache that settles in your bones. You are helpless. And as a mother, that kind of helplessness feels unbearable.

WHY DID YOU LET MY DAUGHTER GET POISONED?

Fear, Blame, and Learning to Trust God with my Child

I can't tell you where I was when I found out. I don't remember the exact moment or even who told me about it. But I do remember the feeling. It was heavy. Like a silence that pressed down on my chest and stayed there. At the time, I already had a son with special needs, and now I was being told that my daughter had lead in her system.

Lead poisoning.

TV and news reports make it sound like the worst thing imaginable. Violent outbursts, developmental issues, and uncontrollable anger. And then suddenly, I was staring down a new fear: raising two children who would both need me in ways that I didn't feel equipped for. The weight of that hit me hard. I couldn't help but blame myself. I was her mother. Wasn't I supposed to protect her from things like this?

I knew exactly where the exposure came from. My parents were having new windows installed in their house, and like we often did, we sent the kids over there while we went away on a short vacation. It felt normal, and familiar. After my daughter's first birthday, she had to go back for routine bloodwork. Nothing out of the ordinary. But what came next shifted everything for us. Her lead levels were elevated. Suddenly, the place we thought was safe, the house we lived in and the house I had grown up in, was now the source of her exposure.

But it didn't matter how or when it happened. My mind went straight to survival: *How do I fix this? How do I keep her safe now, while still living in the same house?*

From that point on, I was on edge constantly. I didn't want her crawling on the floor or touching anything near the windows. I was terrified by her simple playing, exploring, and doing the normal things kids do. My mom and I did everything we could, from taping up walls to wiping windowsills and washing curtains, but the fear was never far off. Every time she went near the curtains or looked out the window, I panicked.

There was one time that she pulled the curtain and started giggling underneath it. I screamed. Louder than I meant to. Because all I could see was danger. She froze, terrified. I had scared her so badly that she started crying, and I broke down right there with her. I pulled her close and sobbed, "I'm sorry." I didn't know how to keep her safe without hurting her emotionally in the process.

She never appeared sick. That made it even harder. She looked fine. She played, laughed, and hit all her milestones. And yet, I was falling apart inside. It was like living next to a ticking time bomb that never went off. But I still had to brace myself for the explosion every single day.

That anxiety stayed with me for years. I held my breath until she turned five or six, always waiting for the day I could finally exhale. They said after a certain age, lead affects children less. So, I waited. I watched. I hovered. Always afraid and always questioning.

For a long time, that house stopped feeling like a home. It became a place I was trying to control, trying to clean, and trying to survive in. But no matter how much I wiped or taped or yelled, I couldn't undo what had already happened.

And I couldn't stop blaming myself.

HOW CAN GOD WANT MARRIAGE IF THIS IS IT?

Wrestling with God's Design and My Reality

I always thought marriage would fix everything. I truly believed it. I thought marriage came with favor, that once I said "I do," God would open the floodgates of peace and joy and steady sunlight that would warm every part of my life. I imagined that marriage would be the turning point I desperately needed — the thing that would settle me, stabilize me, and eventually heal me. I convinced myself that the issues we carried into the relationship would somehow evaporate simply because we exchanged vows. I was sure that love, commitment, and God Himself would smooth out every flaw.

I believed in the fairytale, not the Disney version but the Church version — the one where people said, "Marriage is ordained by

God," and, "When you do things the right way, blessings follow." So I did it. I got married. I tried to do it "God's way." But what I walked into didn't look anything like God. And when things fell apart, I didn't question Him. I questioned me.

Even early on, something inside me whispered that God wasn't in this union the way I hoped He would be. My husband believed in God, yes. He went to church, yes. But only because I went. While I worshiped, he watched videos on his phone. While tears streamed down my face during altar calls, he slept in the pew. That stayed with me in ways I didn't yet know how to name. Deep down, I was afraid to admit that I felt spiritually alone beside the person I had chosen to build a life with. I kept telling myself, "God didn't want this. I forced it. I pushed for the wedding, not the covenant."

I wanted the ceremony, the union, the stability, the picture of God's design — but I wasn't prepared for the weight of what that really required. I had desire, but I did not have foundation. And the truth is, I didn't know how to build one. I thought love would find its own footing. I thought effort would make up the difference. I thought prayer would hold up what maturity, healing, and compatibility could not. But cracks don't close just because you ignore them, and storms don't stop just because you pretend you're prepared.

Still, I was terrified to say any of this out loud. No one had to shame me for wanting to leave; the shame was already alive in my own thoughts. The messages I had absorbed for years kept replaying: divorce is a sin, God hates divorce, marriage is for better or for worse, you need to stick it out. So I stayed. Even when staying felt like drowning with a smile on my face. I didn't know if I stayed because I still loved him or because I was scared — scared that leaving would add another sin to my growing list, scared it would be the final strike that disqualified me from God's grace, scared He would never bless me with another spouse, scared that choosing myself meant I was choosing wrong.

I didn't realize how much fear was shaping my theology. I knew how to fear God, but I didn't know how to trust Him. I didn't know that God's heart for marriage doesn't require you to disappear inside of it. I didn't know that "for better or for worse" didn't mean "for broken and for bruised." I didn't know that covenant and captivity are not the same thing.

But that understanding came later. In the moment, I clung to what I thought God expected from me because I didn't know Him well enough to understand what He didn't.

Looking back, I realized I had never heard anyone teach about the kind of marriage I was living in. People said marriage was "hard work," but no one ever described the kind of hard work that makes you lose yourself. No one explained that you could be married and still afraid to speak, or that you could share a roof with someone and still feel painfully alone. No one told me that a vow doesn't guarantee intimacy or safety. So, I carried that silence, and I carried the guilt, trying to make something sacred out of something that was already fractured.

During that season, I found myself looking at other people's marriages — sometimes strangers on social media — and wondering why mine couldn't look like theirs. I didn't even want their life; I just wanted to feel seen the way they seemed to be seen. The smiling photos, the matching outfits, the little captions about prayer and growth and partnership… even though I knew most of it was curated, it still stirred longing in me. I wasn't jealous of their perfection. I was desperate for their peace.

Most of the marriages I witnessed up close didn't resemble anything I wanted to imitate. But the ones that looked calm, the ones that looked safe, the ones that had softness in the way they looked at each other — yes, I wanted that. I wanted companionship that didn't leave me feeling smaller. I wanted partnership that didn't make me feel like I was carrying everything alone. I wanted love that didn't require me to shrink.

Instead, I found myself holding everything inside. I tried opening up at times — tried to confide in someone, tried to let someone see the truth — but every time I got close to support, it slipped away. Sometimes people drifted. Sometimes conflict came out of nowhere. Sometimes relationships just dissolved. And slowly, I noticed a pattern: whenever someone got close to the truth of what was happening in my marriage, they didn't stay long. Whether intentional or not, my husband found ways to isolate me, to remove the mirrors that could show me what I didn't want to face.

So, I learned to be quiet. Silence became my normal. And with every unspoken truth, the marriage felt heavier. With every moment I swallowed my voice, I felt further from the girl who once believed God would bless this union simply because she tried to honor it.

In the quiet of that season, a painful question kept circling, one I didn't want to confront: how could God want marriage if this is what mine had become? How could something described as holy feel so hollow? How could something meant to reflect Christ's love leave me feeling so unseen, unheard, and undone?

I carried that question for years before I learned the truth — God didn't design marriage to break you. But sometimes we step into things before we're healed enough, whole enough, or aligned enough to carry them. And even then, God's grace still meets us in the places we thought He would never show up.

I CHEATED. I YELLED. I WASN'T THE VICTIM OR THE HERO.

Owning My Part in the Brokenness and Facing Shame

I cheated. Six months into my marriage, I opened a door I could never close. I don't even remember why I did it, not fully. I just know I wasn't getting what I thought I needed. I felt neglected, invisible, and unimportant. I was a wife who didn't feel like one. I was looking to my husband to make me feel whole, but he couldn't do that. Honestly, I couldn't do it either. Neither of us had the skillset for marriage. We wanted the title but weren't ready to carry the weight. Everyone wants a wedding. No one wants to be married.

But I was still the one who cheated.
And it destroyed me.

I remember crying for hours after it happened. I couldn't go home and face the man I had just betrayed. I wanted to stay with my best friend that night, because I knew she wouldn't judge me. But my husband wouldn't allow me to stay the night with her. He told me that I had to come home. I had already sentenced myself, and I really didn't need anyone else's voice adding to the shame.

The next day, while we were running appointments for couples (we were coordinating weddings), he asked me if I cheated on him. I couldn't lie. He already saw me as a liar. And lying again wouldn't fix anything. I told him yes. I told the truth out loud and felt my body crawl. The shame sat at the back of my throat like vomit.

He kept asking questions. Some in the car. Some later at home. I didn't want to answer any of them, but I did. And once I did, nothing was ever the same. He attempted to have sex with me the same day, which was the day after I cheated. When we did, it was… different. The mechanics were there, but the soul of it wasn't. We eventually got back into a rhythm, at least physically, but the marriage itself was truly fractured. Something deep had broken, and we couldn't pretend it hadn't.

I didn't cheat again after that. Not physically. But I didn't heal either. I changed, and not for the better. I became more cautious and more reserved. I didn't entertain men. I barely spoke to them. I only kept a few who were safe to be around—guys who were married or deeply committed to someone else. I knew those lines wouldn't be blurred.

But emotionally and mentally, I was wrecked. I sabotaged

everything I touched. I rejected myself before anyone else could. I didn't feel worthy of love, and I didn't want to be seen. I wore sweatpants and T-shirts almost every day, with most of them being my husband's. Before marriage I was vibrant. I wore colors, did my hair, and I cared. After I cheated, I slipped into a version of myself that looked like a shadow. I saw myself disappearing, and honestly, I didn't try to stop it.

I expected verbal attacks, and I braced myself for emotional blows. I didn't even look at people while I was driving. I would keep my head straight and eyes focused. If a man approached me, I told him to run away because I genuinely felt like my husband was lurking somewhere behind me, ready to shoot him. That is how deep in survival mode I was. That is how twisted my reality had become.

And yes—he used the cheating against me. Constantly.

Every fight found its way back to that night. Every disagreement carried the weight of that betrayal. He thought I was cheating even when I wasn't. With people that didn't even make sense. One time, he thought a client had feelings for me. I told him he was being ridiculous—until after our divorce when that same client admitted he did like me. I was so appalled that my ex-husband had been right, I cursed the man out. I was furious. Not just with him, but with myself.

The truth is that my husband never really trusted me. Even before I cheated. But once I did, I gave him all the ammunition he needed. I confirmed every suspicion. I fed every fear.

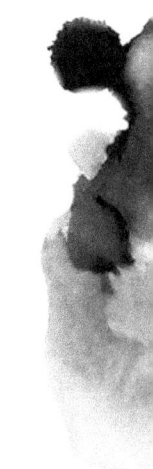

After a while… I went numb. Not because I didn't care, but because the pain became too familiar. I just waited for the next outburst. I stopped trying to defend myself. I accepted the verbal attacks because I believed I deserved them.

My marriage was probably doomed before we even said, "I do." We were both unhealed, both unready, and both clinging to a fantasy that didn't have a foundation. But cheating didn't just kill the marriage. It destroyed the way we saw each other.

And even worse—it destroyed the way I saw *myself.*

That one moment of weakness took over my identity.
It whispered lies into every room I walked into.
It chained itself to my name.

THIS MARRIAGE IS KILLING ME...

Living in a Home of Chaos, Silence, and Survival

I never thought marriage would look like this. Painful. Embarrassing. Defeating.

I didn't grow up dreaming of standing in a kitchen where the silence was thick and the tension was louder than the words. I didn't imagine arguments that escalated until someone was always left wounded either mentally, emotionally, physically, or spiritually. But that was my reality.

Anytime we got into it, things went too far. There was no pause and no retreat. There was always damage. Things said that couldn't be unsaid and things done that couldn't be undone. I remember one of the worst days. Our two oldest sons and our youngest daughter were upstairs. We started arguing again, and I told my husband that I wanted out. I was done. I called the police. Every time I told him I was leaving, he would block the doors, take my keys, and trap me inside. He tried to grab the phone out of my hand. We started wrestling. I slapped him in the face with the phone and tripped over a chair. That was the moment. He called his mother. The police came. And even though I was the one trying to escape, I was the one who almost went to jail. His face was swollen. My actions crossed a line. So, I told them, "Take me. I'd rather sit in jail for a few days than stay one more moment in this house."

That wasn't the only time. A few weeks before that, we had another fight. He slapped candy out of my hand trying to be smart, and his hand accidentally hit my face. Before that? Christmas Day. We got into it again. I was the aggressor that time. I didn't touch him, but I knocked everything over in our room and shifted the mattress off the boxspring. He slammed me into the boxspring, and my leg was bruised for weeks.

Another time, I told him I wished he would die.

What kind of wife says that to her husband?

The kind that's drowning. The kind that's damaged. The kind that's never been taught what real love looks like. We were both unhealed. Both unprepared. Both walking into marriage with trauma, pride, and no foundation. It was a war zone in that house, and not just with each other. We were fighting demons. I am not talking fantasy or fiction. I am talking about the spiritual war, and the kind of torment that started in our thoughts and twisted everything we tried to build. I don't know what was being whispered in his mind, but I know what was whispered in mine,

"You're trapped." "You'll never be free." *"You'll never be safe."*

And I believed it. I felt imprisoned. I don't even know why. The doors were open. I could have left. But somehow, I also couldn't. I loved my kids. I loved my husband. But I felt like I was being held hostage. To be honest, I wasn't just fighting him, I was also fighting me. The brokenness in me. The confusion in me. The girl in me who had never been healed before trying to become a woman and a wife. He was fighting too. With abandonment issues. With deep insecurities. With his own childhood wounds and the ghosts of past relationships. I didn't help. I was always running. Always threatening to leave. Always half out the door.

When things were good, they were good. But when things were bad? They were exceptionally horrible. At least in my head. I couldn't see how to fix it. And truthfully? I didn't want to. I was unwilling.

Every day in that house felt like survival. I would wake up, and on some days, I'd believe I was okay. But I was always on edge. Walking on eggshells. Silencing myself. I couldn't really be a mother to the children. I could only do what he allowed. He made it clear that he was the boss, and that I wasn't really their mother. That they were his kids — not ours.

That crushed me. But then I'd repeat those same words back to him whenever he tried to hold me accountable. I was confused. I went from being pregnant to having four kids. From living with one child to parenting three more. Everything changed fast, and I had no space to process it. If I complained, I didn't love them. If I said I was overwhelmed, I was ungrateful. So, eventually I shut up. Our home became quiet. We didn't talk. We just existed. Watching TV. Breathing the same air but not sharing the same heart.

I became afraid to speak. Because anything I said would be remembered, thrown back in my face, and twisted into a weapon. I started to believe something was wrong with me, and that the way I thought was off. That I was broken in some strange way that no one could understand. I felt like I didn't belong... anywhere.

And I hid. I stopped talking around people, whether they were his friends, my family, or the few friends I was allowed to keep. I tried to hide what was happening. But my husband didn't. He told everyone. He exposed all of it — my faults, my failures, and my flaws. Never his own.

So, I became smaller. Even quieter. Just trying to survive. But survival doesn't last forever. Something had to give. And here's the thing most people don't understand: The moment I decided I was done with the marriage wasn't the moment it ended.

I left on February 15, 2020. But I kept coming back for the kids. For the idea of family. For the hope that maybe, somehow, we could still work. Every few months, we tried again. Counseling. Therapy. Rebuilding. He moved on, and I did too. I was bouncing between him and another man I deeply admired. But that man wasn't any better. No physical abuse, but emotional manipulation. At the time, I couldn't see it. The final straw wasn't something my ex did. It was me.

We were trying again — one more time — and I started overlapping my husband and the other man. I was disrespecting the very marriage I claimed to want to fix. And I had to face that.

I told myself, *If I can't respect this marriage enough to separate the two, then I need to dissolve one.*

I didn't want to hurt him anymore. I didn't want to be the source of more chaos. We had already gone through enough. It wasn't just about letting go of *him.* It was about letting go of who I had become. The chaos. The cycles. The confusion.

> I had to face the truth:
> We were both part of the destruction.
> We both caused damage.
> But I was the only one I could change.

> And I couldn't play another part.
> I had to part ways.
> To face myself.
> To find out what was really going on inside of me.

To stop dying in the name of something that never had the foundation to live.

LEAVING HIM FELT LIKE LEAVING GOD

Divorce, Condemnation, and the Fear of Eternal Punishment

I used to think that getting a divorce meant I was going straight to hell. Not figuratively—literally. In my mind, I was certain that once I died, that was it. Eternal fire. Torture. A devil with horns, grinning as he dragged me into flames because I had messed up one too many times. I truly believed this was my "one and done"—that there would never be another chance at love, never another shot at being seen as worthy. I told myself: You ruined it. You're done. You can still raise your kids, you can still breathe, but don't expect anything good anymore.

That is what divorce felt like. Not just the end of a marriage. But the nail in the coffin of my soul. I didn't want to leave just for me. I wanted to leave for my children. Because what my husband and I were doing to each other, it was messing our kids up. We were showing them chaos, anger, dysfunction, and pain. And I remember thinking that I wanted more for them.

I wanted them to see real love one day. True love. But even as I walked out, a part of me whispered, "You don't get that anymore. Not after this."

After I separated from my husband, I was distracted by a young man I'd been dealing with. It wasn't love, but it was an escape. When he stopped talking to me for a few months, though, that's when it hit hard. That is when the silence screamed. I thought about going back to my husband, not because I wanted him back, but because I was so afraid of what I had just done. But he had already made up his mind. He told me he was done, and he held to that. I couldn't blame him. I had been in and out of his life since day one. And I knew—deep down—that door was closed.

That silence? That lonely space in between? That's where God started pulling me. I didn't feel holy. I didn't feel worthy. But I started seeking. I started paying attention.

Still, I was a mess. I went back to the young man. We had sex again. But something started to change. I couldn't shake the feeling that things were no longer the same. Sex didn't feel the same. The distractions didn't strike me like they used to. God wasn't letting me stay numb anymore.

By the time the divorce was final, something in me had shifted. I didn't feel proud, and I didn't even feel fully relieved. I felt like a statistic. A divorced Black woman with two baby daddies, living in a city where that's the narrative too many times over. I had already felt like a statistic before then. In that moment I just felt like even more of one. Like proof of everything society said I would be.

I remember feeling like that marriage was my punishment. That God had given me that husband and that life as payback for all of the dirt I'd done to other people. Abortion. Cheating. Lying. Rage. Envy. Lust. Laziness. Fornication. Stealing. Unforgiveness. The highlight reel of my sins played on repeat in my head. And I truly believed, that was what I got. That chaos and heartbreak. That heaviness. That was my get-back.

When I finally left, I felt like I was just stacking another reason onto the list of why I deserved hell. I didn't talk to God. Not because I didn't believe He was real, but because I didn't think I was His type. I didn't think He wanted to hear from a woman like me. I wasn't living right. I wasn't making the right choices. I felt like the kind of person God didn't bother with.

I don't remember the words I told myself during that time. But I do remember the feeling. That sick, heavy belief that I deserved everything I was going through. That I had forfeited my shot at joy, peace, and love because of everything I had said and done.

At that time, I was lost.

Not rebellious. Not wild. Just… lost. Walking through a divorce, dragging every sin I had ever committed behind me like anchors. Believing the courtroom was just another confirmation that I had failed too deeply for God to redeem. But even in all that darkness, even when I didn't feel Him, and even when I didn't pray, I realize now that God never walked away from me.

But I'll get to that later. Right now, I'm still telling the truth about the storm.

BROKE, ALONE, AND STILL BREATHING

When Survival Became Surrender and God Provided Anyway

There were seasons where I couldn't even say I was surviving. I was simply still breathing. Nothing more and nothing less. I was separated, raising my children on my own, and holding onto faith by a thread. There were days I felt invisible. Days I'd pray for just one thing to go right. And it felt like life was silent.

I was working full-time as a contract recruiter, but it was commission only. If nobody got hired, I didn't get paid. One year I made $15,000. Another year? Just $11,000. I had people under me, but the commission from them was crumbs. My bills were due, and my kids were growing, but my pockets weren't.

But pride has a way of dressing up survival. I never told my parents how bad it was. I would ask for help only when it was truly the last option. Otherwise, I wore my strength like armor.

I smiled. I kept going. I figured out meals while I juggled bills. I did what mothers do—whatever it takes. I'll never forget sitting one day on the edge of my bed, staring at my daughter's clothes. She had more legs than she had pants. And my son? He needed new shoes, badly. His father, though present, offered the bare minimum. About $5,000 a year in child support. That doesn't go far when you're raising a teenage boy and a growing girl in the city, where kids are cruel, and clothing can be the difference between confidence and ridicule.

I felt defeated. Not just as a woman, but as a mother. I wanted to give them more. I wanted to give them everything. And all I had was barely enough.

So, I cried. I broke for a moment on the edge of that bed. I told God I didn't know what else to do. I had done all I could. I tried it my way. And clearly… my way wasn't working.

That's when the shift began.

It started quietly. Me listening to the Bible increasingly. I wasn't just going through the motions anymore, but instead, I was actively seeking. I was learning how to pray, and how to really talk to God. Once I got the hang of it? Whew. Nobody could tell me anything. Prayer became my power. Surrender became my strategy. God had my full "yes."

I wasn't angry with Him. I was submitted. I stopped pretending I had it all figured out. I stopped acting like I was in control. And something beautiful happened when I let go.

God started to show me He'd never let me down.

Right in the middle of my lack, He reminded me I had never gone without. That I had never been forsaken. That my kids had never missed a meal, had never gone cold, had never had to beg. He'd always made a way even if it wasn't on my preferred schedule. One day in the middle of that surrender, my cousin called and told me about a Goodwill store with "$2 Thursdays." I didn't have much, but I had two dollars. I went in, not knowing what to expect, and I mean... I *cleaned up*. My kids were fully dressed and ready for the new school year. And I had tears in my eyes, because only God could have orchestrated that.

That was a "*Come Through God*" moment.

It wasn't flashy. It wasn't loud. But it was holy. And I celebrated it with everything in me. Because I had cried over pants... and God answered with provision. I had cried out in fear... and God met me with sufficiency. The more I looked back, the more I saw Him in every corner of my struggle. He was the strength I didn't realize I was leaning on. He was the breath that kept me moving when I felt like I was drowning. He was whispering, saying, "Keep going. I got you."

And then He gave me a vision.

He showed me that He wasn't just rescuing me, but instead He was preparing me to serve others. The same way He had provided for me in secret, He would one day use me to pour back into others publicly. That was the revelation that turned the page for me. That was when I knew I was no longer just trying to survive. I was stepping into a new season.

At that time, I was broken and alone… but still breathing. Taking everything one day at a time. Watching God walk me faithfully, and lovingly, into something greater.

Part Two

WHEN GOD STARTED WHISPERING BACK

I WAS PLAYING WITH GOD

Performing Religion while Avoiding True Relationship

I was playing with God.
No, really!
Playing in His face.

Doing things that I knew He wasn't okay with. Pushing the line, crossing it, and then acting like it wasn't that deep. Telling myself things like, "At least I still go to church," or "Other people do worse." I justified my choices so smoothly that I almost convinced myself that God was okay with them too.

But deep down, I knew better.
I just wasn't ready to do better.

I was performing. Playing at church. Playing at being Christian. I could say the scriptures, but I couldn't tell you where to find them. I lifted my hands in worship but didn't lift my Bible to study. I listened to my pastor, but I didn't hear God. I prayed…

but only when I needed something. When my life was falling apart. It was survival-based faith, not an honest relationship.

I looked spiritual on the outside, but I was numb inside. Disconnected, distant, and drifting.

If I'm being honest... at that time I didn't really want to get close to God. Because deep down, I thought I had to fix myself first. Be more consistent. Be more pure. Be more... holy. I thought God only wanted the cleaned-up version of me.

But I was far from clean. I was out there spiraling.

I had cut off all my beautiful hair. I was giving my body to someone who said he loved me, but it wasn't a Godly kind of love. It was carnal. Flesh-driven. He was in love with what he could do with me, not who I was becoming. But I held onto him like he was my peace, because he was the only comfort I had at the time. And even though I wasn't mad at God, I had completely pushed Him to the background of my life.

I knew this life was my fault. God told me not to marry my ex-husband. I heard Him clearly. I heard the "no" and still said "yes" because I thought marriage would fix everything. I ignored His voice, and now I was just dealing with the consequences.

I figured I had made my bed, so I had to lie in it. Might as well try to be comfortable in the chaos. So, I stayed where I was. Pretending. Smiling. Posting. Performing. But I was drowning on the inside.

Then something shifted.

God didn't yell at me. He didn't force anything. But He started to gently get my attention. There were nights I woke up out of my sleep, repenting from dreams and revelations He showed me. Moments where I was reading the Word and something would hit differently. Whispers in my spirit that made me pause and wonder if He was still pursuing me, even then.

I wasn't fully listening yet… but I was starting to hear Him again.

In November 2022, I told God that I was done having sex. I felt Him calling me into abstinence, not out of shame, but to pull me into alignment. And I meant it. But that didn't mean I was instantly holy. By January 2023, I had caved. I went back to the young man, thinking that maybe it would be different. I thought the sex would feel like it used to. That the rivers would flow like milk and honey!

And… nothing.
It was dry.

Literally, physically dry. But also spiritually, and emotionally too. God had dried up my well.

That is when I knew He was done playing with me.

I didn't even feel shame. I just felt clarity. God was making it clear: "This isn't what I have for you anymore." That moment confirmed everything. I said, "Okay Lord… I surrender. You win."

But let's not act like I got it together overnight.
I didn't go cold turkey at first.

I turned to masturbation, thinking, "This is harmless, right?"

But God convicted me. Not through guilt. Through gentle conviction. He showed me that what I called "harmless" was still a form of self-reliance. Still rooted in trying to comfort myself without Him.

Within 30 days of that decision, I threw away every toy. And if you know, you know. That was major.

That was my declaration:
"I'm not going back. I'm not pretending. I'm not playing anymore."

And then God showed me something that changed everything:

He didn't want the perfect version of me. He wanted me. The messed up me. The tired me. The confused, insecure, emotionally wrecked version of me. That's the one He was after. For so long, *religion* had me thinking God only loved me if I did everything right. But *relationship* taught me that He loves me because He's good. Not because I am.

And you know what helped me the most?
Reading the Bible for myself.

When I opened Genesis and started reading, I literally sat there like, "What kind of ghetto mess is this?" These people were wild! Cheating. Lying. Sleeping around. Murdering and manipulating.

They were the ones God used?!

That is when it hit me. The Bible wasn't full of perfect saints. It was full of people like me. And God didn't shun them. He didn't hold grudges. He wasn't petty or distant. He loved them, and He stayed nearby. He worked through their mess and still called them His. That is when I stopped performing and I started pursuing.

Because I finally believed this for myself:
God actually wants me. And He's not scared of my mess.

I DIDN'T FEEL HOLY, I FELT TIRED

Spiritual Dryness and Learning that Obedience is Choice, Not Feeling

Everybody around me was crying, shouting, and falling out. The worship team was going in. The atmosphere felt electric. People were speaking in tongues, hands lifted, eyes closed, tears running.

And me?
I was just clapping.

> Not because I wasn't grateful.
> Not because I didn't believe in God.
> But because honestly… **I didn't feel anything**.

> I just felt tired.

Tired of pretending. Tired of wondering what was wrong with me. Tired of watching everyone else look "on fire" while I sat there feeling like the Holy Spirit skipped over me and moved on to the next row. For a long time, I thought something was broken in me. I thought that maybe I wasn't as saved as *I thought I was. Maybe I missed it. Maybe I wasn't chosen like everyone else.*

It's wild how church culture can make people feel like they don't belong in the room. You have to cry a certain way, or dance a certain way, or speak in "the heavenly language." If not, God hasn't fully accepted you yet. Like the Holy Spirit is some contagious emotional wave to be caught. But let me share what I had to learn:

The Holy Spirit isn't a cold. People don't catch Him.
He's not something that floats around the room looking for hype. He lives inside — in believers in Christ, He's already there.

But in those days, I didn't know that. I was still untangling what I thought a relationship with God was supposed to look like. I had played church for so long that I didn't even know what genuine worship felt like. Honestly, I wasn't trying to fake it anymore, either. I had done that already. I didn't want to pretend to feel moved, and I didn't want to mimic what I saw other people doing. I didn't want to shout if it wasn't real. So, I stayed still. I stayed quiet. And I stayed honest. Authentic.

That might not have looked "spiritual" to some folks, but I knew that God respected it. Because at least it was real.

I spent so much of that season watching everybody else. Comparing my walk to theirs. Wondering, *"Who else is pretending like I used to?"* or *"Who's really worshipping, and who's just performing like I used to?"*

God had to check me:

"You don't know anyone's heart. Only I do."
That humbled me.

I stopped watching them. So, I started watching Him. And even though I still felt spiritually dry... I didn't stop reading. I didn't stop showing up. Because I wasn't doing it for religion, and I wasn't doing it to fit in. I was doing it because I genuinely wanted to know **my Father.**

> And He was speaking.
> Through scripture.
> Through dreams.
> Through conviction.
> Through stillness.

He didn't show up in loud praise breaks. He showed up in quiet, personal whispers. And I have to say those quiet moments held me together... *they really did.*

Here's the thing people don't say enough:

> Even after I stopped pretending...
> Even after I walked away from the lies and the performances...
> Even after I said "yes" to God for real...
> I still felt tired.
> I still felt unsure.
> I still felt like I was not enough.

And that was okay. Because obedience is not about feelings. It is about choice.

I chose Him. Day after day. Not because it felt electric... but because it felt **real**. I still didn't know my full purpose. I was still relearning myself while learning God. Still figuring out how to stop performing and just be **me**. But for once, I wasn't trying to prove anything to anyone. I wasn't fighting to be accepted by people or performance-driven pastors. I was just trying to be present. Open, available, and willing.

What helped?
Community.

Being around like-minded people. Other believers who weren't perfect, but who were actively pursuing. That mattered. They didn't always have the answers, but they had accountability. They reminded me, even on my tired days, that I wasn't alone.

So no, I didn't feel holy. I felt tired. But I stayed committed. Not because of emotion, but because of **decision**.

Because this walk isn't for show.

I HEARD A SERMON... BUT I OPENED MY BIBLE ANYWAY

Discovering God's Truth Beyond Church Noise and Condemnation

For a long time, I thought listening to powerful sermons and showing up to church was enough. I figured if I soaked in enough "good word," I'd automatically get closer to God. But something didn't sit right. Every Sunday felt like I was being beat over the head with hell. The message was always: "Get yourself together or you're going straight to the pit." It wasn't convincing — it was terrifying. It scared me. Even worse, it scared my kids. And I couldn't shake the feeling that there had to be more in this Bible than just condemnation.

I needed answers, and not just reactions. So, I decided to start reading for myself.

To keep myself accountable, I started a Bible study group with the goal of reading through the whole Bible in one year. No, we didn't finish. But we got through a good chunk of it. And honestly, that was enough to change my life. I knew that if I tried to do it alone, I wouldn't make it. I needed the community to hold me steady.

I started in Genesis. Whew. Halfway through, I went upstairs and said, "Daddy, what in the world?! What kind of ghetto mess is this?" He looked at me like, "Huh?" And I said, "Why didn't you tell me this book was based in the hood? Everybody in here is crazy!" He laughed and said, "Wait till you get to the book of Judges."

That was the moment I realized something major: reading the Bible hit completely different than hearing someone preach from it. Preaching gives the highlight reel. Reading provides the raw footage. It helps believers relate. It helps them reflect. It holds a mirror up to life — and not just the polished parts, but the messy ones too.

Let's be clear — the whole book is full of flawed, emotional, reckless people: Samson and Delilah? Irritated my soul. Why would someone reveal their weakness to someone else who is clearly trying to manipulate them?! And then, boom. The Philistines snatch him, blind him, and make him a slave. Sir, are you crazy?!

Jacob and Esau? Flawed.
Rachel and Leah? Flawed.
Rebekah and Abraham? Flawed.
And yet — God used **every single one** of them.

That changed something in me. If God used people like that, people with issues, attitudes, drama, and trauma, maybe He could use me too. I didn't feel like I had to pretend anymore. I wasn't reading about perfect people being loved by a perfect God. I was reading about broken people being redeemed by a faithful one.

The Word started becoming part of my rhythm. I would listen to the Bible at night while I slept. I figured if demons were lurking, they'd get uncomfortable and bounce when they heard Scripture. It became my atmosphere. Even in my exhaustion, even in my confusion, I wanted God around me. During the day, I'd have what I called my "morning dates" with Him. I would drop the kids off, sit in the car, and just talk to God. Not in polished, churchy prayers. I would simply be like, *"What's up, Father? I got questions about the Book of John because… what is happening right now?"*

One day, I was doing a Bible plan on forgiveness and divorce. I was still battling guilt over my own divorce. It haunted me. The shame, the failure, and the feeling of being disqualified from God's love. I read a verse and just broke. I sat in my car and started crying. Telling God, "I didn't know. I didn't know." But the more I read, the more grace I found. I realized I was feeling conviction, not condemnation. And there's a difference.

> *"There is therefore now no condemnation to them which are in Christ Jesus." —Romans 8:1*

In that moment, God didn't throw my sin in my face. He covered me with grace. He reminded me that I was forgiven, even in my ignorance. That I wasn't too far gone. That He wasn't done with me.

That moment shifted how I saw God, and how I saw everything else! I stopped viewing God as if he were a warden and I was the prisoner. Instead, I started viewing Him through truth. Through Scripture, I saw that He is:

- **Love** (1 John 4:8)
- **Merciful** (Ephesians 2:4)
- **Gracious** (Psalm 116:5)
- **Compassionate** (Psalm 145:8)
- **Slow to anger** (Exodus 34:6)
- **Faithful** (Deuteronomy 7:9)
- **Forgiving** (1 John 1:9)
- **Near to the brokenhearted** (Psalm 34:18)
- **A refuge** (Psalm 46:1)
- **The lifter of my head** (Psalm 3:3)

And once I began to see God clearly, I also began to see **me** clearly. Not as a failure or a mistake, but as someone **He chose.**

As someone **He redeemed.**

In Christ, **I am:**

- **A new creation** (2 Corinthians 5:17)
- **Forgiven** (Colossians 1:13–14)
- **Chosen** (1 Peter 2:9)
- **Loved** (Romans 8:38–39)
- **Set apart** (Jeremiah 1:5)
- **Adopted into His family** (Ephesians 1:5)
- **More than a conqueror** (Romans 8:37)
- **His workmanship** (Ephesians 2:10)

And my past? As shameful and heavy as it felt, **He wiped it clean.** He didn't hold it against me. He didn't shame me. He covered it with His blood and set me free.

> *"If anyone is in Christ, they are a new creation.*
> *The old has gone, the new is here."*
> *— 2 Corinthians 5:17*

Reading the Bible changed my identity. I didn't have to pretend that I was perfect. I just had to walk with Him. Flaws, questions, tears and all.

> *"As far as the east is from the west, so far has He removed*
> *our transgressions from us."*
> *— Psalm 103:12*

THIS IS WHO I WAS, I DON'T LIVE HERE ANYMORE

Confessing Sin, Naming Shame, and Rising into Grace

I used to think silence would save me. That if I didn't speak about what I had done and who I had been, then it wouldn't define me. But silence doesn't heal. It hides. And hidden things don't disappear. They decay. Rotting in the dark until either shame consumes you or grace resurrects you.

This was my resurrection chapter.

Not a highlight reel. Not a cleaned-up version of my story. This was the truth. The dirt. The sin. And the scandal of a Savior who didn't flinch when He saw it. A Savior who didn't walk away from my mess, but instead, He walked into it.

I'm not ashamed to say who I was anymore. Because Jesus didn't just clean me up. He raised me from the dead.

I Was a Murderer

I had abortions. Not once. Twice. I ended lives that God had begun. I chose fear and control over faith. I called it "not ready." I convinced myself. But I knew. I knew.

> "You shall not murder." —Exodus 20:13

> "For You created my inmost being; You knit me together in my mother's womb." —Psalm 139:13

> "Before I formed you in the womb I knew you." —Jeremiah 1:5

It took years before I could call it what it was. **Murder.** And saying that word nearly choked me. But naming it was the first breath of healing. I can't bring those children back. I *can* live like someone who knows what grace really costs. I don't live in denial or shame anymore.

I Committed Adultery

I broke my vows and I betrayed trust. I looked for attention, escape, and affirmation in places that never held love. Only momentary relief. Not once, not twice, but multiple times. I became the wound I once bled from.

> "You shall not commit adultery." —Exodus 20:14

I destroyed my soul piece by piece trying to feel alive. But God didn't leave me there. He reached into the rubble and called me back. I don't live in infidelity anymore.

I Spoke Death With My Mouth

I cursed like breathing. I lashed out and humiliated people with my words. I told my husband I wished he was dead. My mouth became a sword that cut deeper than fists ever could.

> "With the tongue we bless our Lord... and with it we curse people who are made in the likeness of God." —James 3:9

> "The tongue has the power of life and death..." —Proverbs 18:21

I became chaos while trying to silence pain. But God gave me a new voice. A healed voice. Now I speak life. I don't live in rage anymore.

I Held Bitterness Like a Trophy

I kept score. I replayed offenses like highlight reels, and I fantasized about revenge. I smiled on the outside and plotted storms on the inside. Bitterness was my poison and I gladly drank it daily.

> "Let all bitterness and wrath and anger... be put away from you." —Ephesians 4:31

> "Vengeance is Mine; I will repay, says the Lord." —Romans 12:19

But bitterness never protected me. It broke me. And then I laid my weapons down. I don't live in vengeance anymore.

I Raged Against God

I yelled at God. I believed He was punishing me. That He didn't care.

> "How long, Lord? Will You forget me forever? How long will You hide Your face from me?" —Psalm 13:1

> "The Lord is close to the brokenhearted and saves those who are crushed in spirit." —Psalm 34:18

But even in my rebellion, He stayed. He held me when I raged. He listened when I accused. God wasn't my enemy. He was my anchor. I don't live in rebellion anymore.

I Idolized Relationships and Control

I made survival my god. I bowed to pain, to sex, and to control. I stayed in toxic relationships because I feared loneliness more than bondage. I clung to dysfunction like it was safety.

> "You shall have no other gods before Me." —Exodus 20:3

> "Those who cling to worthless idols forfeit the grace that could be theirs." —Jonah 2:8

I thought I could save myself. But I couldn't. I began to surrender. Daily. I don't live in idolatry anymore.

I Lived in Sexual Sin

Sex was my medication. Before marriage. After marriage. During my wilderness. It made me feel wanted. Seen, but never whole. I gave away pieces of myself to people who never asked for my soul. Just my body.

> "Flee from sexual immorality… you are not your own; you were bought at a price." —1 Corinthians 6:18-20

> "It is God's will that you should be sanctified: that you should avoid sexual immorality." —1 Thessalonians 4:3

It didn't heal me. It hollowed me. Finally, my body began to belong to God. I don't live in compromise anymore.

I Was Proud, Pretending, and Spiritually Dead

I smiled while breaking. I served in church but didn't know the God I claimed to represent. I had religion but no relationship. I wore strength like a mask and died underneath it.

> "Having a form of godliness but denying its power." —2 Timothy 3:5

> "These people honor Me with their lips, but their hearts are far from Me." —Matthew 15:8

God didn't want my performance. He wanted me. So, I gave Him everything. I don't live behind masks anymore.

I Believed I Was Too Far Gone

I thought I was too dirty. Too complicated and too guilty. I didn't see hope, I just saw damage. But God saw destiny.

> "Come to Me, all who are weary and burdened, and I will give you rest." —Matthew 11:28

> "Where sin increased, grace abounded all the more." —Romans 5:20

I was never too far.
Neither was anyone else.

I Stopped Living There

I used to live in guilt.
But I began to live in grace.
I used to wear shame like a name tag.
Then I learned to wear His righteousness like a crown.

> "If anyone is in Christ, he is a new creation. The old has passed away; behold, the new has come." —2 Corinthians 5:17

> "For you were once darkness, but now you are light in the Lord. Live as children of light." —Ephesians 5:8

That was who I was. But I stopped living there a long time ago. I'm not who I used to be. I continued to heal, continued to grow, and remained surrendering, but I was resurrected.

> *And if God can raise someone like me—He can raise you too.*

Part Three

REAL PEOPLE. REAL SINS. REAL REDEMPTION.

THEY DON'T PREACH ABOUT THE REALNESS OF THE REAL ONES

Messy Saints who Prove God Uses the Broken

When we think about the people God used in the Bible, we often imagine saints glowing with perfection. People who had it all together. But if we really open the Bible and read it for ourselves, not just the Sunday school stories or the polished sermons, we see something so much messier and so much more human. The truth is, God's chosen ones were often deeply flawed. They were liars, adulterers, murderers, doubters, and outcasts. And yet, God called them anyway. He met them right in their mess and used them for His perfect will.

Church often highlights the big victories in religious history.

The giant slain, the sea parted, and the walls that fell. But they rarely speak about David's lust and murder, or Rahab's life in prostitution, or Peter's denial in the middle of Jesus' most painful night. We hear the surface-level victories but miss the raw, broken roads that led to those moments. We're left thinking we have to be perfect before God can use us. But the Bible tells a different story.

David wasn't just a king after God's heart; he was a man who let his desire lead him to murder an innocent man. Rahab wasn't just a woman who hid the spies; she was a prostitute living on the margins of society. Peter wasn't just the rock upon which the church would be built; he denied even knowing Jesus three times. Paul wasn't just a preacher to the nations; he was a violent persecutor who hunted down Christians. These people didn't start out clean. They didn't get chosen because they had it all figured out. God chose them in their imperfection to show us that His grace can reach the deepest, darkest parts of us.

When I started really reading the Bible, I realized it wasn't a book about perfect people doing perfect things. It was a book about broken people being met by a perfect God. It is a story of redemption and grace. It tells a story that shows us God isn't scared of our sin or surprised by our failures. He doesn't wait for us to clean ourselves up before He steps in. He wants us as we are so that He can transform us and show His power through our weakness. When I have felt like my past disqualified me or that my mistakes make me unworthy, these stories prove otherwise. God didn't call the qualified; He qualified the called. He used their pain, their past, and their weaknesses to write the most beautiful stories of victory. And He wants to do the same with us. He wants to take our mess and turn it into a message, to take our breakdown and turn it into a breakthrough.

This chapter is an invitation to see ourselves in these "real ones." To stop thinking we're too far gone, too broken, or too flawed. Because the same God who called them is calling us. And He's not asking us to be perfect; He's asking us to be WILLING.

DAVID WAS A MESSY LOVER & A MURDERER

From Lust and Murder to Worship and Redemption

We can stop sugarcoating it: David was messy. Beautifully, brutally, biblically messy. His story is the kind we don't hear preached in full, not because it isn't powerful, but because it's too real. Too human. Too much like us. But if we're going to talk about God using broken people, then we need to talk about all of David. Not just the giant-slayer, but the woman-taker, the murderer, the griever, and the man who worshipped with tears on his face and blood on his hands.

1. Chosen While Overlooked
David's story didn't begin with a crown. It began

with rejection. When the prophet Samuel came to Jesse's house looking for the next king of Israel, Jesse paraded all his sons before him, except for David. He was out in the field with the sheep, forgotten by his own father. But God told Samuel,

"Man looks at the outward appearance, but the Lord looks at the heart." —1 Samuel 16:7

That's where it started — not with perfection, but with heart.

That part of David's story speaks to those of us who've been overlooked, uninvited, and left out. Those who were picked last. Those who were never seen as "the one."

2. The Giant Slayer

We love the Goliath part. David, a boy with a sling, stepping into battle when grown men backed down. It was faith in raw form. He told Goliath, "You come to me with sword and spear… but I come to you in the name of the Lord." And he won. Not because of his strength, but because of his confidence in God.

That moment in David's life shows the high. The faith-filled fire. I have had those moments too. When I believed God could do the impossible. When I had nothing but hope and a little "sling" of faith. We all have giant-slaying moments. But we also have cave seasons…

3. Running, Hiding, Surviving

After David's anointing, he didn't go straight to the throne. He went through years of being hunted like a criminal. King Saul, threatened by David's favor, tried to kill him. David hid in caves. He ran for his life. He even pretended to be insane in front of enemies just to survive (1 Samuel 21:13). People talked about him. Lied on him. He lost friends. He lost comfort. He lost any semblance of normal. Some of us know that season well.

4. The Sin with Bathsheba

Here comes the part most churches skip over — or tiptoe around.

David saw Bathsheba bathing. He wanted her. So he sent for her and slept with her, even though she was married to Uriah, a loyal soldier in his army (2 Samuel 11). She got pregnant. David panicked. He tried to cover it up by bringing Uriah home, hoping he'd sleep with her and think the baby was his. But Uriah, loyal to his fellow soldiers, refused. So David did the unthinkable. He had Uriah killed. He sent him to the front lines and made sure the army pulled back so he'd be struck down.

Then he married Bathsheba like nothing happened.

How many of us know what it's like to try to cover our sin? To clean up a mess with a bigger mess? I have done it. Lied to cover a lie. Slept with someone to forget someone else. Hurt people to hide how broken I felt inside. Like David, I've tried to fix sin with more sin. But we can't cover what God wants to heal.

5. The Confrontation and the Consequence

God saw everything. He sent the prophet Nathan to call David out. Nathan told a parable about a rich man stealing a poor man's only lamb, and when David got angry about the injustice, Nathan said, "You are that man." (2 Samuel 12:7)

David was wrecked. He realized the depth of what he had done. As a consequence, God allowed the child created from the affair to die. David fasted, prayed, wept, and begged God to spare the baby. But the child still died. And after the baby's death, David did something powerful. He got up, washed, and worshiped.

That part hit me deep. Because I know what it's like to cry out to God and not get the answer I hoped for. I have fasted and I have wept. I have begged and bargained. And still, things died. Relationships, dreams, and peace. But like David, I learned to worship through the loss.

6. The Restoration

God didn't leave David there. After all the failure, pain, and death, God gave David and Bathsheba another son: Solomon. The one who would become the wisest king and build God's temple. God took something broken and created legacy out of it.

That's what grace does.

Despite everything, the lust, the lies, and the murder, God still called David a man after His own heart. (Acts 13:22) Not because he never sinned. But because he never stayed in it. David's psalms are proof: "Have mercy on me, O God…", "Create in me a clean heart…", "Restore to me the joy of your salvation…" David sinned hard, but he repented harder.

Why This Matters Now

David's story is not just Bible history. It is a mirror. Because today, we still have Bathsheba moments. We still try to cover things up. We still fall, lie, break promises, and run from accountability. But grace is still available.

God doesn't love us less because of our worst chapter. He just wants us to bring it to Him. If God can use David with all his baggage, then He can use any of us. If He can write worship songs through the mouth of a murderer, then what could He do through our pain? I am not proud of everything I've done. But I am proof that God doesn't give up on the messy ones. He redeems us. Restores us. Uses us.

> *"Create in me a clean heart, O God; and renew a right spirit within me." — Psalm 51:10*

RAHAB WAS WORKING THE STREETS... AND STILL GOT IN

A Prostitute Written into Jesus' Bloodline

L et's talk about Rahab, the woman most churches either rush past or sanitize. By not doing that, however, it was possible to look at her exactly as the Bible presents her: a woman who sold her body to survive, who was looked down upon by society, and who still made it into the bloodline of Jesus.

Yes. That Rahab. The one with a past.

1. Rahab's Reputation

Rahab was a prostitute. Not in secret. Not "former" or "recovering." She was a woman with a label, and everyone in Jericho knew it. In that culture, being a prostitute meant being considered less than human. Something to be used, shamed, whispered about, and avoided. Not someone to be seen with, much less be saved through. But that's exactly what God did.

In today's world, Rahab wouldn't be welcomed in most churches.

She would be side-eyed for what she wore. Dismissed because of what she did to survive. Written off as someone who "should've known better." And yet, she's still written into God's eternal story. That hit me. Because I've worn labels too. Maybe not the same one, but they carried the same weight. I was the girl with kids from different fathers. The one who walked away from her marriage. The one who made messy choices with her body, her heart, and her mouth. I didn't feel chosen. I felt judged.

But like Rahab, God saw me differently.

2. Rahab's Risk

When the Israelite spies came to Jericho, Rahab didn't hesitate. She hid them on her roof and lied to protect them (Joshua 2). Think about that: she risked everything for a God she had only heard about.

She wasn't part of Israel. She didn't grow up learning the Torah or going to temple. She just heard the stories. About the Red Sea, the plagues in Egypt, and the victories God gave His people. She believed in Him enough to take action.

That kind of faith? That is raw. That is brave. That is real. Not church-taught, but born out of desperation and trust.

She told the spies,

> *"I know that the Lord has given you this land...*
> *the Lord your God is God in heaven above and*
> *on the earth below." —Joshua 2:9-11*

That was her confession of faith. And God honored it. I remember when I first started truly seeking God. I didn't have all the answers. I was still broken, still battling shame, still unsure if He'd even want someone like me. But I came anyway. I prayed anyway. I opened my Bible anyway. I acted in faith, right in the middle of my mess. Just like Rahab.

3. The Scarlet Cord

Before the spies left, they made Rahab a promise. She would be saved, along with her family, if she tied a scarlet cord in her window as a sign (Joshua 2:18). That scarlet cord? It symbolized safety, covering, and faith. When Jericho's walls fell, everything crumbled except the part of the wall where Rahab's home stood (Joshua 6:22-23). Everyone else perished. But she lived. Why? Because she believed.

In my life, there were times when everything around me fell apart. Relationships, finances, family, and my health. But like Rahab's house, I stayed standing. Not because I was strong, but because I tied my own "scarlet cord." Faith in a God who knew me, loved me, and wouldn't leave me behind. That cord wasn't perfection. It was trust.

It wasn't religion. It was relationship. That is what saved her. That is what saved me.

4. Rahab's Legacy

This is where the story gets wild. God didn't just save Rahab and move on. He grafted her into the family. She married Salmon, an Israelite, and they had a son named Boaz. Yes, the one who married Ruth. And from that bloodline came King David… and eventually, Jesus Himself (Matthew 1:5).

The prostitute from Jericho became a great-great-grandmother of the Messiah. What kind of God does that? A God who rewrites shame. A God who flips the script. A God who sees faith where others only see failure.

Why This Matters Today

Let's be real: today's world still throws labels.

"Single mom."

"Too many kids."
"Too sexual/Hoe."
"Too loud/Ghetto."
"Too broken/Unhealed."

But God's not looking at the label. He is looking at our heart.

He doesn't call us by our past. He calls us by our potential. Rahab didn't wait until she was cleaned up to move in faith. She moved in the middle of her reputation, and that is what made her so powerful. If Rahab could go from the red-light district to the royal lineage and be used to protect God's people, save her family, and be honored in Scripture… then so can we.

We don't have to be spotless. We just have to say yes.
We don't have to fit into a church mold. We just have to trust.

"By faith the harlot Rahab perished not with them that believed not, when she had received the spies with peace." — Hebrews 11:31

If He let Rahab in, He's letting us in too.
Not because we're perfect.
Because we're *willing.*
And because He loves us more than our history could ever disqualify us.

SAMSON HAD STRENGTH... BUT NO DISCIPLINE

When Gifts are Wasted by Compromise, and Grace Restores

L et's talk about Samson, the man with God-given strength but a weakness that ran deeper than any muscle could protect. We hear about him as the strong man of the Bible. The one who killed a lion with his bare hands, took down an army with a jawbone, and pulled down a temple with his final breath. But if we stop there, we miss the point. Because Samson's story wasn't just about strength. It was about the slow fade of a man who couldn't control his desires. It was about someone anointed but still ruled by the flesh.

If I'm honest... that is a lot of people... including me!

1. Set Apart — But Still Struggling

Samson was chosen before birth. He was set apart as a Nazirite, a person dedicated to God. That meant no alcohol, no touching dead things, and no cutting his hair, all outward symbols of an inward calling (Judges 13). God's Spirit moved through Samson powerfully. He was born with purpose.

But being called doesn't mean we are guarded. And anointing without discipline will always lead to destruction. Some of us know what that's like. We were called. Gifted and anointed. But still drawn to people and things that chipped away at our purpose. Samson didn't fall all at once. He fell in stages. One compromise at a time.

2. The Women, the Warning Signs, and the Wounds

Samson had a pattern. He kept falling for the wrong kind of women. First a Philistine woman his parents warned him about (Judges 14), then a prostitute (Judges 16), and finally Delilah. The one who would take him down completely. Each woman didn't just bring pleasure. They came with warning signs, but Samson ignored them. Delilah wasn't subtle. She asked him repeatedly to reveal the secret of his strength. She was working with his enemies, and she betrayed him repeatedly. But Samson stayed. He laid in the lap of someone who was sent to destroy him.

Let that sink in.

How many of us have laid our heads in laps we had no business in? People we knew weren't safe, but we stayed. We saw the red flags and ignored them. We let someone hold what was sacred.

We gave away our secrets. We kept going back. We thought it was love, but in fact it was bondage.

Delilah didn't break Samson's vow. He gave it away.

3. The Fall
After telling Delilah the truth, that his strength was tied to his hair and the symbol of his Nazarite vow, she shaved his head while he slept. When the Philistines came to capture him, the Bible says one of the most chilling things:

> "He did not know that the Lord had
> left him." —Judges 16:20

That verse hurts. Because sometimes we don't realize how far we've drifted until the consequences show up. Until we are caught. Until we are empty and we are bound. Samson was seized, his eyes were gouged out, and he was thrown into prison. He went from called to chained... because he followed his feelings instead of his purpose.

4. The Redemption
But here's the beauty of God's grace. Even after Samson lost it all, the strength, and the vision, and the freedom, God wasn't done. In that prison, his hair began to grow again (Judges 16:22). That little sentence is everything. It means the vow wasn't void. It means restoration was possible. And when Samson humbled himself and cried out to God one last time, he was given strength again. Not for himself, but for God's purpose. He brought the

temple down, defeating more of God's enemies in his final act than he had during his entire life. He died in repentance. He died remembering who gave him the strength in the first place. God honored that.

Why This Matters Now

We live in a world full of Delilahs. People, habits, addictions, and patterns that will lull us into compromise. Many of us, like Samson, have already laid our heads down. We have given our energy, our faith, and our peace to things that don't serve God's purpose for us. But it's not too late.

Even if we've lost our strength. Even when we've been left broken, blinded, and bound by our own choices. If our hair is growing again, and if our faith is coming back, and if our desire to seek God is waking back up — then grace is still working.

Samson reminds us:
- Being called doesn't make us immune to falling.
- Falling doesn't mean we're finished.
- Repentance can restore what compromise stole.

> *"And Samson called unto the Lord, and said, O Lord God, remember me, I pray thee, and strengthen me, I pray thee, only this once..." — Judges 16:28*

Our strength isn't gone — it's just growing back.

God's not through with us. Even if we gave too much to the wrong people. He still hears our cry. He still honors repentance. And He can still use us, even in our final hours, to bring glory to His name.

PETER ACTED LIKE HE DIDN'T KNOW JESUS

Denial, Shame, and the Breakfast of Restoration

Peter's story is one of the most relatable, chaotic, and grace-soaked journeys in the entire Bible. He was loud. Emotional. Messy. He got it so right one moment, and then so wrong the next. But through it all, God never let go of him.

If we were being honest? A lot of us are Peter.

1. The Call: From Fisherman to Follower

Peter wasn't a priest. He wasn't educated, and he wasn't respected. He was a fisherman. Just a blue-collar, rough-around-the-edges, cuss-when-he's-angry kind of guy.

But one day, Jesus stepped into his boat, taught the crowd, and then told Peter to let down his nets once again. After catching so many fish the nets began to break, Peter dropped to his knees and said,

> *"Depart from me, for I am a sinful*
> *man, O Lord!" —Luke 5:8*

Jesus didn't argue. He didn't say Peter wasn't sinful. He just said, "Follow Me, and I'll make you a fisher of men." And Peter did. He dropped his nets and walked into destiny.

That spoke to me. God didn't wait for Peter to be cleaned up, dressed up, or spiritually educated. He called him just as he was. Like me, like us, Peter was chosen right in the middle of his ordinary, messy, and insecure life.

2. The Zeal: All Heart, Little Restraint

Peter went hard for Jesus.

He was the first to say,

> *"You are the Christ, the Son of the*
> *Living God" —Matthew 16:16*

He was the one who jumped out of the boat to walk on water. (Matthew 14) And when the guards came to arrest Jesus, Peter drew his sword and cut off a man's ear! (John 18:10) He was passionate, but impulsive. He had boldness, but not always wisdom. He loved Jesus... but didn't always listen to Him.

That reminded me of my earlier walk with God. When I was

zealous, but untrained. On fire, but not consistent. Talking big, but not always backing it up.

Peter was a "real one" — messy but loyal. Flawed but fervent.

3. The Failure: Denial, Cursing, and Bitter Tears

When Jesus told His disciples He'd be betrayed and crucified, Peter said, "Even if I have to die with You, I'll never disown You." But a few hours later, Peter couldn't even admit he knew Jesus. Three different times, people asked, "Aren't you one of His followers?"

And the last time:

> *"Then began he to curse and to swear, saying, I know not the man." —Matthew 26:74 (KJV)*

The rooster crowed. Jesus looked at him.
And Peter broke.

That moment wrecked me. Because I know what it's like to say, "God, I'll never go back," and then go back anyway. To promise change and fall again. To stand for God in private but shrink in public. And when the guilt hit? It crushed me.

Peter wept bitterly. But God wasn't done.

4. The Grace: Breakfast on the Shore

After Jesus rose, He could've gone to anyone. But He made a point to go find Peter. On the shore of Galilee, Jesus cooked breakfast for His disciples (John 21). He looked at Peter, the denier, and asked him three times:

"Do you love Me?"

Each time Peter answered yes, Jesus said, *"Feed My sheep."* That's redemption. Jesus didn't bring up the denial. He brought up the calling.

God restored Peter with grace. He replaced shame with mission. He didn't just forgive Peter, He entrusted him.

5. The Power: The Same Mouth that Denied... Preached

On the day of Pentecost, it was Peter who stood up. Peter, the one who once cussed and denied Jesus, preached boldly to thousands (Acts 2). 3,000 people were saved.

The same mouth that said, *"I don't know Him,"* now shouted, *"Repent and be baptized in His name!"*

Peter became a leader in the early church. He healed the sick, faced persecution, and refused to stop preaching the gospel. Eventually, he was sentenced to death. And tradition says Peter asked to be crucified upside down, feeling unworthy to die the same way as Jesus.

What a transformation. From fisherman to failure to faithful shepherd.

Why This Matters Now

Peter's story is for all of us who have ever:

- Started strong but failed miserably
- Made bold promises and broken them
- Chosen fear over faith
- Denied God with our lives
- Thought we blew our chance at being used by Him

We are *still* called.
We are *still* loved.

God can use the same mouth, the same story, the same life you thought disqualified you. To preach, to lead, and to testify.

> *"Then began he to curse and to swear, saying, I know not the man…"* That was Peter. But later?

> *"Repent, and be baptized… and you will receive the gift of the Holy Spirit."* — Acts 2:38

That was Peter too.

We are not just our denial — we are also our return.

We are not just our breakdown — we are our comeback. God isn't looking at who we were by the fire… He's waiting for us at the shore.

JACOB & ESAU — LENTILS, LIES, AND LEGACY

Family Dysfunction, Wrestling with God, and a New Name

L et's be honest. This story is a whole soap opera. It is full of family favoritism, impulsive decisions, betrayal, lies, heartbreak, and revenge. In other words… it sounds just like real life.

Jacob and Esau weren't just twin brothers, *they were also rivals.* Their story shows what happens when emotions run high, when people get desperate, and when families fail to love fairly. But more than that, it shows what God can do even through the dysfunction.

Because sometimes the most beautiful legacies are born in the ugliest beginnings.

1. Esau Traded Legacy for a Lunch

Esau came in from the field hungry. Starving. Dramatic. He saw Jacob cooking a pot of lentils and said, "I'm about to die — give me some of that stew."

Jacob, always calculating, said, "Sell me your birthright first."

And just like that, Esau gave up his future for a bowl of food (Genesis 25:29-34).

Let that sink in.

The birthright meant leadership, blessing, inheritance, and spiritual authority. He gave it all away for temporary satisfaction.

We still do that today. I've traded peace for pleasure. Purpose for people. God's promise for my own timing. We have all had moments where we gave up something valuable to feed something immediate. And like Esau, we didn't realize what we lost until it was too late.

2. The Lie That Broke a Family

It didn't stop there. Rebekah, Jacob's mother, favored him over Esau. And when Isaac grew old and blind, Rebekah devised a plan:

"We'll dress you in Esau's clothes. We'll make your arms hairy. You'll go in and pretend to be him. Your father will bless you instead."

And Jacob did it. He lied multiple times. He said, "I am Esau." He even used God's name to sell the lie (Genesis 27:19-20). Isaac, though hesitant, eventually believed him and gave him the blessing. When Esau came in later and realized what had happened, he was devastated. He wept and begged his father, "*Bless me too, my father!*"

But the blessing had already been spoken.

That part hurts because some of us have felt robbed too. Robbed of love. Robbed of opportunity. Robbed by family. Whether through favoritism, abandonment, or dysfunction, many of us grew up in homes where things weren't fair... and it left scars.

3. Running, Reaping, and Wrestling

Esau was so angry he vowed to kill Jacob.

So, Jacob ran.

And where did he end up? In the house of his uncle Laban, who turned out to be just as slick as him. Jacob worked seven years to marry Rachel, but on the wedding night, Laban gave him Leah instead. He had to work another seven years just to marry the woman he truly loved (Genesis 29). Jacob got a taste of his own deception — he reaped what he sowed.

But even in that mess, God was with him. Struggling through the consequences of our own mess? Facing people just like the parts of ourselves we try to hide? That was Jacob. And many of us were Jacobs, too.

4. The Wrestle That Changed Everything

Years later, God told Jacob to go home. But going home meant facing Esau, the brother who once wanted him dead. Jacob was terrified. He sent gifts ahead. He divided his camp. He planned for the worst.

But the night before the reunion, something happened. Jacob was alone. And a man, God in human form, came and wrestled with him all night (Genesis 32:24-30). This wasn't a polite prayer or a gentle conversation. It was a fight. Jacob was wrestling for a blessing.

And when the man tried to leave, Jacob said,

"I will not let You go unless You bless me."

So, God touched his hip and left him limping but also gave him a new name:

Israel, meaning "one who struggles with God and prevails."

Jacob went into that night as a deceiver. He came out of it with a limp… and a legacy. I have wrestled with God. In grief and in guilt. In confusion, I've cried out, *"Why did You let this happen?"*

"Why am I like this?"

"Why does my family look like this?"

And still, in the wrestling, He showed me I was more than my mistakes. More than my upbringing. More than what I lost.

5. The Reunion: Grace in the Arms of the One He Hurt

The next morning, Jacob limped toward Esau expecting revenge. But what he got instead was forgiveness. Esau ran to him, embraced him, and wept (Genesis 33:4).

That's grace.

Esau had every right to hate him. But he hugged him instead.

Some of us are still running from the people we hurt. Still avoiding hard conversations. Still expecting judgment…but God's working on both sides of the story.

Why This Matters Now

This story is about family wounds, dysfunction, manipulation, and mercy. It shows us:

- We can be both the victim and the one who caused pain.
- God can still use us, even if our story is full of wrong turns.
- Sometimes the greatest breakthroughs come through the biggest wrestles.
- A limp isn't a curse — it's a reminder that we survived, and God renamed us.

We might come from a broken family. We might have lied, stolen, manipulated, or given up our blessing for a quick fix. But God still has a name for us. And He's writing our legacy in ink. Not pencil. There is no erasing what He's ordained.

> *"Thy name shall be called no more Jacob, but Israel: for… thou hast prevailed."* — Genesis 32:28 (KJV)

We are not the sum of what we've done. We are the result of who He called us to be.

And even if we walk with a limp… we're walking in destiny.

THOMAS – DOUBT, PROOF, AND A NEW DECLARATION

How Jesus Turned Skepticism into the Boldest Confession of Faith

Thomas gets a bad name.

"Doubting Thomas."

Like he was the only one who ever needed proof. Like we all don't have days where we question everything we thought we believed. But the truth? Thomas wasn't a weak disciple. He was a wounded one.

1. He Walked with Jesus… and Still Had Questions

Thomas wasn't some kind of outsider. He walked with Jesus for three years. He left his old life. He followed. He listened and he believed. He watched

Jesus open blind eyes, raise the dead, cast out demons, and feed thousands with scraps.

He wasn't new to the Faith. He was invested. And that's what made his heartbreak so real. Because when we have given our whole heart to something, and it falls apart, everything gets shaken.

Thomas watched his teacher, friend, and Savior get arrested like a criminal. He saw the One who healed others get beaten and bleed out. He watched hope die on a cross, and his faith crumbled with it. We don't talk enough about that kind of faith-loss. Not from rebellion, but from trauma. From seeing things happen that we never expected God to allow. I've been there. It isn't that I didn't want to believe. I just didn't want to get my hopes up and be disappointed again. That was Thomas.

Honestly? That is a lot of us.

2. "Unless I See It..." — The Honest Confession

When the other disciples told him, "We saw Jesus! He's alive!", Thomas didn't celebrate. He didn't shout hallelujah.

He said,

> *"Unless I see the nail marks in his hands and put my finger where the nails were... I will not believe." — John 20:25*

He didn't say that because he was petty. He said it because he was in *pain*. He had believed once and it broke his heart. He wasn't trying to be difficult. He was just being *real*. And God honors *real*.

I have prayed those prayers too:

"God, unless You show me something…"

"Unless I hear You clearly…"

"Unless You help me right now, I don't know how much longer I can keep going."

I didn't need a sermon. I needed a sign. I didn't need spiritual language. I needed a real encounter. Just like Thomas.

3. Jesus Came Back Just for Him

Eight days passed. Thomas sat in his pain. And then Jesus showed up… again. He had already appeared to the others. But this time He came specifically for the doubter. Not to scold him. Not to shame him. But to invite him.

Jesus walked through the door, looked straight at Thomas, and said,

> *"Put your finger here. See my hands. Reach out and touch my side. Stop doubting and believe." —John 20:27*

Thomas broke. He didn't need a lecture. He just needed a moment. He fell to his knees and said,

> *"My Lord and my God!" — John 20:28*

That was the most powerful declaration of Jesus' divinity in the whole Gospels. It came not from Peter, and not from John. It came from the one who doubted most.

That told me something:

God can turn your doubt into your declaration.

He can meet you in the exact place of your fear and build your greatest faith from it.

I have had moments where I said, "God, if You're real, I need You to meet me in this."

And He did. Not always how I expected. But always in the way I needed.

4. Thomas the Missionary — Not Just the Doubter

We don't talk enough about what happened after that moment.

Thomas didn't stay the "doubter." He became one of the boldest missionaries of the early church. Church tradition says he took the gospel all the way to India, spreading the name of Jesus across continents. He didn't just recover his faith. He ran with it. He died a martyr, refusing to deny Christ.

His story didn't end with doubt. It ended with devotion.

Why This Matters Now

We may be in a place where faith feels shaky. Where we want to believe again, but we're afraid to hope. Where we've been burned by people, church, or life. Where the silence from heaven feels deafening, and we find ourselves saying, "*Unless I see it…*"

I get it. And so does Jesus.

This story proves:

- God is not afraid of our questions.
- He's not threatened by our doubt.
- He will show up for the brokenhearted, even if it's eight days later.
- Our honesty doesn't push Him away, it draws Him closer.

> *"Thomas, because you have seen Me, you have believed. Blessed are those who have not seen and yet have believed." — John 20:29 (KJV)*

That's us. Those who didn't get to see the nail-scarred hands in person. But we still believe. Even through tears and even through trauma. Even with questions.

We are not our doubt. We're still His disciples.
Even when our faith is cracked... *He's coming back for us.*

Part Four

I'M STILL NOT PERFECT.
BUT I'M NOT
GOING BACK.

YOU DON'T HAVE TO BE PERFECT TO PURSUE GOD

Choosing Relationship over Religion and Daily Surrender

People keep telling us that we have to get it all together before we come to God, but that couldn't be more wrong. I really believed that all the sex I was having disqualified me. The way I cussed people out like it was second nature. How I treated people was cold, harsh, and guarded because I was protecting my own heart. My anxious, spiraling thoughts and PTSD felt like chains. I carried all of that and thought, "Why would God want me?" I felt filthy, unworthy, and fully convinced that I had to fix myself first before I even dared to approach Him.

But as I kept seeking Him, piece by piece and prayer by prayer, something started to shift in my spirit. I realized that even if I thought He didn't want me, I still wanted Him. And the more I read, the more I saw that He did want me, mess and all. Seeing the broken and flawed people in the Bible made it click. David was a whole mess. Peter denied Jesus and cursed people out while trying to distance himself. Paul literally hunted Christians down. Yet, God loved them and used them and called them by name. That realization connected me to Him in a way I had never experienced before.

That connection felt just like how I love my own kids. No matter how wild they act, no matter how badly they mess up, there's absolutely nothing they could do to make me stop loving them. That's exactly how God loves us. He's not sitting there waiting for a spotless version of us to show up. He wants the raw, real version.

Once I accepted this truth, everything started shifting. Not overnight, but day by day, the way I walked changed. The way I talked changed. Even the way I thought about myself started to transform. I still didn't get excited about the big "church worship shows" because sometimes they felt more like performances than genuine moments with God. But in my car, in my room, and when I was with my people who love Him, that's where it got real. That is where I felt His presence the most. My daily choices shifted too. Who I hang out with, what I was watching, what I listened to, and what I let influence my spirit. I wasn't moving to impress anyone anymore; I was moving because I loved Him and wanted to honor Him for real.

When we feel too dirty or too far gone, we need to hear this: we're exactly who God wants. We might not believe that in the moment — I didn't believe it at first either. But just try Him. Start learning about Him even if it feels awkward or forced. No need for fancy words or a perfect script. Just talk to Him like talking to a best friend: "God, I don't even know what I'm doing, but I'm here." I promise, He will meet us exactly where we are. And slowly, we'll start to see peace sneak in. The mornings will feel a little lighter, and the weight will start to lift.

James 4:8 says, "Draw nigh to God, and he will draw nigh to you." That means come close. Messy, raw, and undone, and He'll come running to us. Isaiah 1:18 reminds us, "Though your sins be as scarlet, they shall be as white as snow." He's saying, "I can handle it all. Just come to me."

We don't have to fix ourselves first. We don't have to hide. We just have to show up. Honest, messy, and open, and let Him do the transforming only He can do.

> *"Draw nigh to God, and he will draw*
> *nigh to you." — James 4:8 (KJV)*

STAND.
EVEN IF YOU'RE
STANDING
IN TEARS

Perseverance in Pain as an Act of Faith

Ever been in a season so heavy that the only response was to stand there, tears rolling down your face and legs shaking, with a mind questioning everything? But still standing? I have. I didn't run. I didn't sit down and let it wash me away. I stood, because somewhere deep inside, I believed there had to be more beyond that moment.

Standing isn't just about surviving. It is about believing in a promise even when it can't be seen. It is saying, "God, I don't know how You're going to fix this. I don't know how I'm going to get through today. But I trust You more than I trust my feelings."

That trust isn't pretty. It is not always strong. Sometimes it's the quietest, most fragile whisper we've got left. But it's still trust. I have had seasons where standing felt like the last thing I could do. When I lost jobs and didn't know how I'd pay my bills. When my marriage crumbled and I felt like a failure. When my ex-husband was murdered. When my son was diagnosed with Autism. When my daughter was lead paint poisoned. But through all those storms, God held me up. Even when my faith was down to crumbs, He met me there and carried me. That's the beauty of our God. He doesn't require us to have it all together; He just asks us to keep showing up.

Ephesians 6:13 says, "Having done all, to stand." That means after we've prayed all the prayers, cried all the tears, and fought every battle, we keep standing on the word of God. Even if we're standing on wobbly legs. Even if our tears are soaking the floor beneath us. Because standing is an act of defiance against the enemy. It is our silent declaration: "I won't give up. I still believe God is who He says He is."

Standing doesn't mean we're fearless. It doesn't mean we're invincible. It means we know that the God who promised to never leave or forsake us is right there in the middle of it with us. He's not waiting for us to get up strong and shout. He's holding us even in our trembling silence. And every time we choose to stand, heaven notices. God honors that quiet, messy courage. God never asked for perfection; He asked for perseverance. He asked for faith the size of a mustard seed, and sometimes standing is the only way to show that faith. Standing shows that we're expecting Him to show up, even when our natural eyes can't see a single way out.

So today, if all we can do is stand — then stand. Stand in the tears, stand in the shaking, stand in the questions. Because even if it doesn't feel like it, that posture is a victory. That posture is worship. That posture is hope.

> *"Therefore take up the whole armor of God, that you may be able to withstand in the evil day, and having done all, to stand." — Ephesians 6:13 (KJV)*

TALK TO HIM. EVEN WHEN YOU'RE MAD.

Real Prayer, Raw Emotions, and God's Safe Presence

S ome of us have been taught to approach God like He's some strict principal in the sky, waiting to punish us the moment we slip up. So when we feel angry, frustrated, or disappointed, we go silent. We act like we can hide those feelings from Him, when in reality, He already knows. He hears the thoughts we never say out loud, the questions we're too scared to voice, and the anger we bury deep. Guess what? He can handle it.

I have had moments where I was mad at God. I didn't scream out loud, but my spirit was tight and closed off.

I felt like saying, "Why do I keep getting the short end of the stick? Why does it feel like every time I take a step forward, I get knocked five steps back?" Those moments felt heavy, and it felt easier to shut down than to open up. But it's in those exact moments that God wants to hear from us the most.

Talking to God isn't about performing. It isn't about hitting the perfect pitch or saying the "right" holy words. It is about relationship. When I started talking to Him like I talk to a close friend, everything changed. I would say, "God, I'm mad. I don't understand. I'm tired. Why does this keep happening?" And He met me right there. Not with lightning bolts of anger, but with comfort, understanding, and sometimes a gentle nudge of conviction.

Psalm 62:8 says, "Trust in him at all times; ye people, pour out your heart before him: God is a refuge for us." Notice that — pour out our heart. Not our filtered, dressed-up heart. Our raw, unfiltered, broken heart. He doesn't just want the pretty pieces. He wants all of it.

We think that holding back protects us, but it actually keeps us from experiencing His fullness. The more honest we are with God, the more we invite Him into those messy spaces. It is in those messy spaces that He does His best work. Those tears we cry alone? He collects them. Those questions that haunt us at night? He hears them. He's not running from our anger or our doubt; He's inviting us to bring it to Him so He can show us who He really is.

Some days my prayers don't even sound like prayers. They sound like conversations, complaints, confessions, and rants. Sometimes just sounds. But that's real relationship. We don't have to censor our feelings before We come to God. He's big enough to handle every single one.

So, talk to Him. Even when we're mad. Even when we're disappointed. Even when we don't have the words to explain what's happening inside. He wants us anyway.

> *God can handle your rawest, ugliest emotions. He would rather hear your honest rage than your silent performance.*

HE STILL SEES US

The God Who Notices Us When We Feel Invisible

K now those moments when we feel invisible? Like no one notices the silent battles we fight or the tears we cry behind closed doors? We can be surrounded by people and still feel unseen. But here's the truth that shifted everything for me: God still sees us.

Even in our mess and even when we're hiding. Even when we feel forgotten, He sees us clearly. Psalm 139:1-2 says, "O LORD, thou hast searched me, and known me. Thou knowest my downsitting and mine uprising, thou understandest my thought afar off." He doesn't just see our actions. He understands our thoughts, our fears, and our private struggles. We don't have to perform for Him. We don't have to dress it up or explain it away. He sees us at our rawest and still chooses to love us.

There were times when I thought I had drifted so far that God must've turned His back on me. I was certain He was done with me. That I had crossed too many lines and broken too many promises. But He never did. He watched me, patiently waiting for me to turn back. He knew every late-night cry, every anxious spiral, every fake smile I wore to get through the day. He saw all the ways I was trying to hold myself together and all the ways I was falling apart. And in all of that, He stayed close to me.

When we know God sees us, it changes how we see ourselves. We stop looking for validation in broken places. We stop chasing love in people who don't know how to give it. We realize that the One who created the stars in the sky knows our name, our struggles, and our story, and calls all of us His. He doesn't just see the highlight reel. He sees the behind-the-scenes footage: the breakdowns, the moments of weakness, the hidden pain. And He loves us deeply anyway.

Think about Hagar in Genesis 16. She ran away into the wilderness feeling used, abandoned, and alone. But God didn't leave her there. He met her in that lonely place and showed her that she was seen. She named Him "El Roi," the God who sees me. In her most desperate moment, when she felt like no one would ever come looking, God showed up and spoke directly to her pain.

Knowing that He sees us brings comfort, but it also calls us to a deeper level of honesty. We don't have to fake strength in His presence. We don't have to pretend to be okay. He knows when we're not okay and invites us to come as we are. He invites us to lay it all down and trust that He's not going anywhere.

So, when you feel unseen, unheard, or unnoticed, remember this: He still sees us. In every mess, in every dark corner, in every hidden tear. And He always will.

You are never invisible to God. He sees every piece of you — and He still calls you His.

"I'D DIE FOR YOU"

How Human Love Failed but Jesus' Sacrifice Proved True Love

When I first met my ex-husband, he told me, "I'd die for you." That line hooked me deep. There's something about someone being willing to give up their life for us that feels like the ultimate sign of love. I held on to those words for so long, thinking they were proof that he was my forever. But what I didn't realize was that those words were just words. When life got heavy and the storms came, that kind of love couldn't hold me up.

Years later, after we had separated, those words came echoing back to me one night: "I'd die for you." I couldn't shake it. Then it hit me like a wave crashing over my entire soul. My ex-husband only promised it, but Jesus actually did it. Jesus didn't bother to say He would die for me; He just died! He let them beat Him, mock Him, pierce Him, and hang Him up on a cross like a criminal. And in those final moments, with every labored breath, He had me in mind. He had all of us in mind.

And here's the wildest part: Jesus didn't have to do it. He could've snapped His fingers and wiped out every person standing against Him. He could've looked at us and thought, "They're not even worth it." He could've called down a legion of angels and left us to face the consequences of our mess. Instead of praying for His Father to take the cup from Him, He could've just said, "Nah, I'm good. I'm coming home. These people are playing in my face." He had every right to walk away. If it was me, I probably would've let everyone get swallowed up by fire and brimstone, turned into salt, or let the locusts tear through the land. But Jesus didn't. He stayed. He chose to love us anyway. He chose to see us as worth it.

We hold so tightly to human love that often fails us. We beg people to stay, to prove their love, to fight for us. But the truth is, most people can't even handle our mess, let alone die for us. Jesus saw every bit of our mess, our secrets, our betrayals, and He still said, "I'll go." That's not some storybook romance. That's raw, real, sacrificial love that no one else could ever match.

John 15:13 says, "Greater love hath no man than this, that a man lay down his life for his friends." Jesus called us His friends, and then He backed up His words with His life. He didn't ghost us when it got hard. He didn't turn His back when we acted up. He didn't walk away when we disappointed Him. He went all the way to the cross.

I spent years holding onto empty promises by men who eventually left. I kept putting my faith in words spoken by broken people instead of the actions of a perfect Savior. When that realization hit me, it broke me open in the best way. It forced me to release my grip on counterfeit love and grab hold of the one love that never changes, never fails, and never walks away.

Some of us are out here waiting for someone to "prove" their love, to take a bullet, or to fight for us. But friend, that proof already exists. Jesus took the punishment none of us could bear. He bore the weight of every sin so that we could have life. And not just life, but life more abundant. Let me also be clear: I am not against marriage. God created marriage. But there's a difference between a Godly marriage and a worldly one. A marriage built on God's foundation is a union meant to reflect His love, grace, forgiveness, and sacrifice. Please don't think that a spouse will never let us down. They will. They are still human, just like us. This is not a marriage book. This is a book about learning who Christ is and how His love changes everything.

We don't have to keep chasing after people to validate ourselves. We don't have to keep performing for love that will leave us empty. We don't have to stay addicted to the pain of false promises. The realest love story was already written in blood on a wooden cross, and it's been waiting for us to see it all along. So today, stop holding on to the hope of being chosen by someone else, and please know — we were all already chosen. We were already worth dying for.

This isn't about being perfect; it's about being present. Keep showing up, even when you feel unworthy. God already decided you were worth it. The cross proves it. Every step you take toward Him, He is already running toward you. You are loved, chosen, and never alone.

THIS AIN'T THE END. IT'S JUST THE BEGINNING

Walking into a New Season of Grace, Purpose, and Hope

We spend so much time thinking our story is over when the bottom falls out. We assume the pain means God is done with us, and that the failures mean we've disqualified ourselves. But hear this clearly: this ain't the end. It is just the beginning.

All those moments that could have been final breaking points? They were actually building resilience. All those closed doors, heartbreaks, and detours? They were detours to something better and something deeper. God doesn't waste a single tear or a single setback. Romans 8:28 reminds us that "all things work together for good to them that love God, to them who are called according to his purpose." Even when it doesn't make sense in the moment, He's stitching together a greater plan.

There have been so many seasons where I felt like I was standing in the ashes of my life, wondering how I'd ever move forward. But God specializes in bringing beauty from ashes. He can turn the ugliest chapters into testimonies that set other people free. He loves to take the broken pieces and build something more beautiful than you could ever imagine. When we realize that this is just the beginning, we start to see our pain differently. We see it as preparation, not punishment. We understand that God's not trying to break us down to leave us, but instead He's breaking us open to rebuild us stronger. We see that every "no" was actually protection. Every heartbreak was redirection. Every loss was setting us up for something we couldn't have imagined.

This isn't about ignoring our pain or pretending it didn't happen. It is about recognizing that God is still writing our story. And as long as we have breath, He's not done with us yet. In fact, He's just getting started. He's preparing us for a new season, a new anointing, and a new level of purpose that is beyond what we prayed for. The scars we carry? They become marks of His faithfulness. The pain we've endured? It becomes the platform for His glory.

So, we stand up. Wipe our faces. Take that next step, even if it's shaky. This isn't the end of our story. It's just the start of a new chapter filled with healing, growth, and new levels of faith we never thought possible. We are walking into a future that is covered by His grace, led by His hand, and filled with His promises.

This is our triumphant moment. Our comeback season. Our proof that God still does miracles, that He still restores, and that He still loves us fiercely. We are not too far gone. We are not too broken. We are exactly who God chose to redeem and restore.

God's not finished. He's just getting started with you. Your story isn't over. Get ready. This is just the beginning.

DEAR READER,

If you made it to the end of this book, I want you to know something straight from my heart: you are not alone. You are not too far gone. You are not forgotten. You have not been left behind. You are not too messy for God to reach down and hold you close.

I know what it feels like to think that you're beyond saving. To stare at the ceiling in the middle of the night wondering if anyone even notices the pain you carry. I know what it's like to feel like the weight of your past disqualifies you from a future with God. I know what it's like to feel like God doesn't care about you anymore. I know what it's like to crack the pages of the Bible open and read nothing but constant convictions and judgment based on the life you're living. I know because I've been there. I've sat in the darkest corners of shame, wrapped up in guilt so heavy I thought I'd never breathe again. I have questioned my worth, doubted my purpose, and wondered if God had turned His face away from me completely.

But here's what I learned: even in my deepest pit, He was there. When I was filthy in my thoughts and in my words, when I ran from Him, when I kept going back to the same mistakes, He stayed. He never stopped calling my name. He never stopped waiting for me to come home. Your story isn't over. Those broken places in your heart? God wants to heal them. Those secrets you swore you'd never tell? He already knows. The nights you cried until your pillow was soaked? He collected every tear. You are seen. You are loved. You are chosen. Still.

Do not let anyone convince you that you have to clean yourself up before you come to God. Don't let religious performance rob you of a relationship with your Father. He doesn't want your perfection. He wants your honesty. He wants your scars. He wants your shaky prayers and your tired hands lifted up in surrender. If all you can do today is whisper "help," that is enough. If all you have is a broken hallelujah, that is enough. If all you can offer is your tears, they are enough.

I wrote this book because I wanted you to see that even in the middle of the ugliest, messiest, most painful seasons, God is still writing your story. He doesn't see you as a lost cause. He sees you as His child. And no matter how many times you've wandered, He's still standing at the door with arms wide open.

Please, don't give up. Don't believe the lie that you're unworthy of love and redemption. You are worth it. You were worth the cross. You are worth the pursuit. I pray that as you close these pages, something inside you ignites. That you would take one more step toward Him, even if it's shaky. That you would dare to believe that maybe, just maybe, God could love someone like you. Because He does.

I love you, and I'm rooting for you. But more importantly, God loves you — deeply, wildly, endlessly.

With all my heart,
Your Sister in Christ

AFTERWORD

If you think this book was written to bash my ex-husband, then you missed the point entirely. That was never the goal of these pages, nor was it ever the posture of my heart. Writing this book was not about shaming him. It was about showing God. Not about highlighting my husband's failures, but instead about highlighting God's grace through my own.

The truth is, I loved my husband. I still remember the moment that it hit me the hardest — it wasn't in the beginning when our love was fresh, or during the years when I stayed hoping things would change. It was in the courtroom at our very first divorce hearing. I sat there with the realization that I couldn't even part my lips to say one negative thing about him. The judge might have been waiting, but I could not bring myself to tear him down. Because deep down, despite the chaos, despite the pain — I still loved him. And that love couldn't be faked. It wasn't for show. It wasn't naïve. It was real.

Now let me be clear: was there domestic violence in my marriage? Yes. Was it wrong? Absolutely. Did I stay? Yes. Longer than I should have. Was staying the right choice? I can't answer that for anyone else, but for me, it was not. And yet, here's a truth that might surprise you: I didn't leave because of the physical violence.

For a long time, I thought marriage was about endurance. Just sticking it out no matter what. I thought love meant swallowing pain, forgiving instantly, and pretending like nothing happened so the house could stay at peace. But love is not silence. Love is not enabling. Love is not pretending. I didn't leave because I stopped loving him. I left because love wasn't ever going to be enough to fix what was broken between us. We both struggled with what marriage was supposed to look like. Neither of us had the foundation we needed. We didn't know how to be husband and wife, and we didn't fully know how to be parents. I can be honest with you…I struggled with parenting for a long, long time. I still do, in some ways. I have had nights where I cried myself to sleep wondering if I was failing my children. And through it all, here I remained. Still pressing. Still praying. Still trying to trust that God was shaping me even when I felt like I was stumbling.

But that's the thing about marriage, and parenting, and even faith; we must walk into these roles without a manual, without a perfect model, and without all the answers. We must try. We must fail. We must try again. We honestly were trying, but we didn't have the foundation to stand on. And when the storms came — the inevitable ones that always come — our house crumbled.

We both knew God. That is the part that stung the most. We knew Him and we both grew up around Him. We heard His Word. But knowing God and keeping Him in your marriage are not the same thing. I want to be crystal clear about what I mean, because some people could read this and assume I was talking about the kind of toxic marriage where one spouse manipulates the other by using God's name as a weapon. You know the kind: "God told me you need to submit.", "God said you're the problem.", "God wants you to do this."

That is not what I'm talking about.

I am not talking about using God as a tool of manipulation. I am talking about genuinely seeking God — both husband and wife — going before Him in humility and asking Him to change them from the inside out, so that their love for each other may reflect His love for all of us. That is what we were missing. Instead of letting God heal us, we tried to heal each other. Instead of going to Him, we went to our own strength. We tried to glue each other back together with apologies and empty promises. We tried to tape over the cracks so that nobody else could see how broken we were. We smiled in the pictures. We showed up at church. We played the part. But inside the walls were crumbling.

Two broken people cannot fix each other. Two wounded hearts cannot stem the flow of bleeding. How can one person in the midst of drowning rescue another person from the same fate?

It simply doesn't work. We both needed God. Not just a Sunday version of Him, and not just a "pray before dinner" version of Him. We needed His presence, His Spirit, and His healing. And without Him, we inevitably failed.

Scripture says, "Unless the Lord builds the house, the builders labor in vain" (Psalm 127:1). That was us — laboring in vain. We were trying to build something in our own strength, and every time we thought it might hold, another storm came and knocked it down. We forgot the most important truth: only God makes us whole.

Unfortunately, my ex-husband is no longer with us. He passed away in January 2025, just one year after our divorce. And that grief...is complicated. People assume that when a marriage ends, the love ends as well. But when he died, I realized love doesn't work like that. Divorce didn't erase the memories we created together. It didn't erase the years we shared. It didn't erase the fact that he was the father of my children. And death has a way of bringing all of that back to the surface. When I heard the news, it wasn't anger I felt. But it also wasn't relief. It was grief. Real grief. Because even though our marriage ended, he was a part of my life, and a part of my story, and his absence would always matter. And I wanted to make sure this book never painted him as the villain. He was human. Like me. Flawed. Like me. Trying. Failing. Falling. Like me.

If anything, his passing reminded me how fragile life is. How short it can be. How unfinished our stories feel when we try to write them without God at the center. It reminded me to forgive quickly and to love harder. To pray deeper. To not let bitterness have the last word. Because tomorrow isn't promised. Not for me, not for you, and not for anyone we love.

So, when I say this book isn't about bashing him, I mean it with my whole heart. I can't bash a man who shaped so much of who I am. I can't erase his role in my story. And I wouldn't want to. Because even through the storms, even through the brokenness, God was writing something greater.

> *"Teach us to number our days, that we may gain a heart of wisdom."* —Psalm 90:1

His story ended sooner than I would have ever expected. But mine is still being written. And so is yours. And if you've carried grief, whether it's the end of a marriage, the death of a loved one, or the death of dreams you thought would live forever, know this: God is still close. Scripture says, "The Lord is close to the brokenhearted and saves those who are crushed in spirit." (Psalm 34:18). I have lived that truth. And I pray you will too.

That is where I want to leave you. Not in my broken marriage, not in the mistakes of my past, but in the wholeness that God offers. Because if there's one thing I want you to carry from this book, it is this: God heals. God restores. God redeems. You may feel shattered. You may feel like your life is nothing but taped-up cracks and glued pieces. But God takes broken things and makes them whole again.

*"He heals the brokenhearted and binds up their wounds."
(Psalm 147:3)*

*"My grace is sufficient for you, for my power is made perfect in
weakness." (2 Corinthians 12:9)*

*"The Lord is close to the brokenhearted and saves those who are
crushed in spirit." (Psalm 34:18)*

*"See, I am doing a new thing! Now it springs up; do you not per-
ceive it? I am making a way in the wilderness and streams in
the wasteland." (Isaiah 43:19)*

This is not just about marriage. Maybe your storm looks different
than mine. Maybe it is parenting. Maybe it is addiction. Maybe
it is grief. Maybe it is financial struggle, or loneliness, or shame.
Whatever your storm is, know this: God still sees you. He still
has a plan. You can still stand.

If my story has shown you anything, I pray it shows you this:
storms will come. You will feel unqualified. You will feel unworthy. But even in your brokenness, even in your weakness, even
in your failures, you are still chosen.

This book has been my testimony, but I believe it's also been
a mirror. Maybe you've seen yourself in my struggles. Maybe
you've seen pieces of your own story in my words. And maybe,
just maybe, you've seen glimpses of God's hand in places you
once thought He had abandoned you.

He never left. He never will. And if you remember nothing else, remember this: God is the only one who can take broken people, broken marriages, broken dreams... and make them whole.

Let me close with this prayer for you:

Father, I thank You for the one who is holding this book right now. You know their storm. You know their pain. You know their doubts, their fears, their hidden wounds. I ask You to meet them right where they are. Heal the brokenhearted. Bind up their wounds. Remind them that they are not forgotten, not forsaken, not too far gone. Show them that even in their imperfection, they are still chosen. Let them walk away from these pages not just with my story, but with Your hope. In Jesus' name, Amen.

This isn't the end of my story, and it isn't the end of yours. It is just the beginning of something new. Keep pressing. Keep praying. Keep trusting. Because even when everything else falls apart, God never does.

SCRIPTURES TO STAND ON

"He heals the brokenhearted and binds up their wounds." —Psalm 147:3

Meaning:

This verse tells us that God pays close attention to people who are hurting. When the Bible says He "heals the brokenhearted," it means God doesn't ignore emotional pain the way people sometimes do. He doesn't say "get over it," "move on," or "it's not that deep." He sees every disappointment, betrayal, loss, heartbreak, trauma, and hidden wound you never told anyone about.

"Binds up their wounds" is a picture. In biblical times, binding wounds meant gently cleaning, treating, and wrapping an injury so it could heal properly. This is God's way of saying, "I am not just aware of your pain — I personally tend to it."

Your emotional injuries matter to Him. Your heart is not too damaged for Him. And healing isn't just a church word — it's what God does carefully and intentionally.

Application:

1. *Bring God the real wounds you're carrying, not the version you pretend is fine.*

   Applying this scripture begins with honesty. In a world that tells you to "move on" or "stay strong," God invites you to acknowledge where you're truly hurting. This may be a broken relationship, a betrayal, grief that lingers, childhood trauma, or even wounds you caused yourself. God heals what you reveal. When you talk to Him openly about your pain, you give Him access to the places that need His touch.

2. *Give yourself permission to heal at the pace God sets, not the pace people expect.*

   Wounds don't close overnight, and neither do hearts. Social media, society, and sometimes even church culture can pressure you to look whole before you actually are. But God binds wounds slowly, carefully, and thoughtfully. Applying this verse means refusing to rush your healing or feel guilty for still being affected by something that hurt you. Healing is not weakness — it's divine restoration.

3. *Pay attention to what still hurts, because that's where God is working.*

   Often, God reveals wounds by allowing certain things to trigger you — a conversation, a memory, a relationship pattern, or an emotional reaction that feels too big for the moment. Instead of judging yourself, see those moments as God gently uncovering where healing is still needed. He is showing you the areas He wants to tend to, not to embarrass you, but to liberate you.

4. *Replace the lies your heartbreak taught you with God's truth.*
   Heartbreak often whispers lies: "You're unlovable," "You're forgotten," "You're not enough," "Your life is ruined," or "You'll always feel this way." Applying this scripture means allowing God to challenge those lies with His truth. If God is healing your heart, then your story isn't over. If God is binding your wounds, then you are not too broken for restoration. Every wound He touches becomes a place of strength.

5. *Partner with God in your healing by taking intentional steps forward.*
   God heals, but He often invites you to participate in the process. This may look like therapy, setting boundaries, journaling, forgiving, taking rest seriously, distancing from toxic environments, or finally acknowledging the pain you've been suppressing. Healing is both God's work and your willingness. When you take steps toward wholeness, you allow God's healing to go deeper and last longer.

Repeat After Me: My wounds are not the end of my story — God is healing every part of me.

"Come unto me, all ye that labour and are heavy laden, and I will give you rest." —Matthew 11:28

Meaning:

Jesus is talking directly to people who are tired — not just physically, but tired in their souls. "Labour and are heavy laden" means people who are overwhelmed, stressed, anxious, burdened by life, weighed down by responsibilities, guilt, expectations, heartbreak, or spiritual exhaustion.

When He says "come unto Me," He isn't asking you to perform, be perfect, clean yourself up, or prove yourself worthy. He's simply saying:

"Bring your tired self to Me. Bring the version of you that is worn out. Bring the version of you that can barely hold on. Come as you are."

"I will give you rest" doesn't mean a quick nap or a vacation. It means He will give rest to your soul — the part of you that never seems to shut off. It's the kind of rest nothing else can provide.

Application:

1. *Be honest about your exhaustion instead of pretending you're fine.*

   Applying this verse means acknowledging where you're tired — emotionally, mentally, spiritually, or physically. In today's world, everyone is performing strength, but Jesus invites you to stop pretending and come to Him with the version of you that feels worn out. Whether the weight comes from family, money, relationships, heartbreak, trauma, anxiety, or simply trying to hold everything together, Jesus wants you to bring that heaviness to Him without fear or shame.

2. *Talk to God about your burdens exactly as they feel, not how you think they should sound.*
"Come unto Me" means bring your raw, unfiltered self to God. You don't need perfect words or long prayers — just honesty. You can say, "Lord, I'm overwhelmed," or "I'm exhausted, and I don't know what to do." God responds to sincerity, not performance. When you tell Him the truth, you make space for Him to give you the rest your soul has been craving.

3. *Let go of the belief that you have to carry everything alone.*
In 2025, we've been conditioned to be independent, self-reliant, and constantly strong. But Jesus is saying, "You don't have to carry this by yourself anymore." Applying this scripture means surrendering the need to control every outcome. It means trusting God with the things that are too heavy for you — the problems you can't fix, the people you can't change, and the situations you can't force. When you release the weight, God fills the space with peace.

4. *Create moments of stillness so your spirit can actually rest.*
Sometimes the way Jesus gives rest is by nudging you to slow down. Rest doesn't always mean doing nothing — it means creating room for your soul to breathe. This may look like setting boundaries, turning off your phone, spending time in scripture, breathing deeply, or simply

sitting quietly with God for five minutes. Rest is not laziness; it's obedience to a Savior who cares about the condition of your heart.

5. *Let Jesus comfort the parts of you that feel overlooked, burdened, or worn out.*

   Rest is not just the absence of stress — it's the presence of Jesus in your stress. When anxiety rises, when fear overwhelms you, when you feel lost or unsupported, remember that rest is not something you have to earn. It's a gift He freely gives to those who come to Him. Applying this scripture means letting His peace replace your pressure, His comfort replace your worry, and His strength carry the weight you can't hold anymore.

Repeat After Me: I don't have to carry this alone — Jesus gives my soul the rest it needs.

"There is therefore now no condemnation to them which are in Christ Jesus, who walk not after the flesh, but after the Spirit." —Romans 8:1

Meaning:

This verse is God's declaration that when you belong to Christ, He does not condemn you. Condemnation means shame, guilt, punishment, rejection, or the belief that you are "too messed up" for God. Paul is saying:

"If you are in Christ, God is not holding your past over your head."

Your mistakes, your sins, your decisions, your failures — those are not chains God uses to keep you in bondage. The enemy condemns. People condemn. You may even condemn yourself. But God does not.

"Who walk not after the flesh, but after the Spirit" doesn't mean you have to be perfect. It means your life is moving toward God now. You're trying. You're seeking Him. You're learning. You're growing. Even if you stumble, even if you fall, you are still walking with Him, not against Him.

This verse is about freedom from shame and freedom to start again.

Application:

1. *Stop Replaying What God Has Already Forgiven.*
   When condemnation tries to sit on your chest and remind you of everything you've done wrong, this scripture gives

you permission to let it go. You don't have to rehearse your mistakes or drag your past into every new season. If God is not condemning you, then you no longer need to keep punishing yourself emotionally or mentally. Every time old guilt rises, speak the truth: God has already released you. You are not defined by who you were; you are defined by who He is in you now.

2. *Recognize the Difference Between Conviction and Condemnation.*

Condemnation tears you down, but conviction corrects you with love. Condemnation says, "You are the problem," while conviction says, "Here's how you can grow." In today's world — where you are constantly exposed to opinions, criticism, and comparison — this discernment is everything. If a thought pushes you away from God, that's condemnation. If it pulls you toward change, humility, and healing, that's conviction. Let conviction shape you, and let condemnation die at the door.

3. *Walk Toward God, Even If Your Steps Are Small.*

Walking "after the Spirit" simply means moving in God's direction. It's not perfection — it's pursuit. In your everyday life, this may look like choosing to pray instead of shutting down, choosing forgiveness instead of bitterness, or choosing to pause instead of reacting out of emotion. Reading one scripture, whispering a short prayer, or guarding your peace is still movement toward God. As long as you are walking forward — even imperfectly — you are aligned with this verse.

4. *Stop Letting People Define You by a Season God*
    Delivered You From.
    Sometimes condemnation doesn't come from you; it comes
    from others who refuse to see your transformation. In 2025,
    when everyone has an opinion and social circles spread infor-
    mation faster than truth, it's easy to feel trapped by who you
    used to be. But God does not hold your past over your head,
    and no one else has the authority to either. You have permis-
    sion to outgrow old narratives, old environments, and old
    expectations. You are allowed to be new.

5. *Let This Verse Silence Every Voice of Shame.*
    Shame will always try to speak louder than grace. It will
    tell you that you're unworthy, unqualified, and unforgivable.
    When that voice rises, Romans 8:1 becomes your weapon.
    Shame has no authority in the presence of God's forgiveness.
    Use this scripture to quiet the internal battles, the insecu-
    rities, and the fears that try to pull you back into bondage.
    Speak it until your spirit believes it: there is now — not later,
    not eventually — no condemnation for you.

6. *Use This Verse as Armor During Emotional or*
    Spiritual Attacks.
    Condemnation often attacks in weak moments — late at
    night, after a mistake, during loneliness, or when memories
    resurface. In those moments, this verse becomes spiritual
    armor. Say it out loud if you have to. Remind your mind, your
    heart, and the enemy that you are covered by Christ. Shame
    cannot sit where God has declared freedom. When you stand

on this scripture, you stand on the truth that nothing in your past has the power to separate you from God's love today.

Repeat After Me: I am not condemned. God has freed me, forgiven me, and called me forward.

1 Peter 5:6 - Humble yourselves therefore under the mighty hand of God, that he may exalt you in due time.

Meaning:

This scripture teaches that humility is not weakness — it's surrender. "Humble yourselves" means choosing to trust God's leadership instead of trying to control everything on your own. It means acknowledging that God sees the full picture while we only see pieces. "Under the mighty hand of God" is a reminder that His hand is both powerful and protective. Being under His hand doesn't mean being pushed down — it means being covered and guided.

"That He may exalt you in due time" means that God has a perfect moment for your breakthrough, your elevation, your healing, and your promotion. When you surrender your need to rush, force, or manipulate outcomes, God promises to lift you up when the timing is right. His timing may not match your expectations, but His timing is always tied to readiness, protection, and purpose.

Application:

1. *Release the need to control everything and trust God's timing.*

   Humbling yourself in today's world often means choosing patience where you want results, choosing prayer where you want action, and choosing surrender where you want control. You don't have to force outcomes, chase validation, or rush into opportunities out of fear of missing out. When you place your desires, timelines, and anxieties under God's authority, you make room for Him to move in ways you couldn't create on your own. True humility is saying, "God, I trust Your timing more than my own urgency."

2. *Accept that God's process often feels slow, but it is always intentional.*

   Humility is not just lowering yourself — it's recognizing that elevation without preparation leads to destruction. In 2025, when everyone is trying to go viral, be seen, or elevate themselves instantly, this verse reminds you that shortcuts come with consequences. God's timing protects you from opportunities you aren't ready for and environments that could crush you. When you feel overlooked or delayed, humility helps you remember: if God hasn't opened the door yet, it means the foundation is still being built.

3. *Stay teachable, correctable, and willing to grow.*

   Humbling yourself means being willing to learn from God, from Scripture, and even from uncomfortable moments. It requires admitting when you're wrong, apologizing when necessary, and allowing God to confront the parts of you that need healing or refining. In a culture that encourages pride and self-defense, humility opens your heart to transformation. When you stay teachable, God can shape you into who you need to be for the next season.

4. *Stop comparing your pace to everyone else's journey.*

   Comparison is pride in disguise — it says, "I should be farther than I am." But humility says, "God is writing my story at the right speed." When you look at other people's accomplishments, marriages, careers, or spiritual growth, it's easy to feel left behind. Humbling yourself under God's hand means believing that your timeline is not broken. God exalts you in your due time, not someone else's. Your delay is not denial — it is divine timing.

5. *Prepare for elevation by being faithful where you are right now.*

Humility pairs with obedience. When you handle what God has placed in front of you with excellence — your job, your children, your healing journey, your spiritual growth — you position yourself for God to lift you higher. In due time, He will open the right doors, bring the right connections, restore what was lost, and elevate you to places your pride could never take you. Humility keeps you ready so that when God says "now," you can step into it with character, strength, and gratitude.

Repeat After Me: Elevation is God's job. Humility and obedience are mine!

Isaiah 48:10 - See, I have refined you, though not as silver; I have tested you in the furnace of affliction.

Meaning:

This verse is God explaining that He uses difficult seasons to purify and strengthen His people, but not in a way that destroys them. Refining silver requires intense heat to remove impurities, but God says He refines you differently — not to burn you, but to build you. "The furnace of affliction" is not literal fire; it represents painful experiences, hardships, loss, disappointments, and the intense pressures of life.

In this verse, God is saying, "I allowed certain hardships, not to punish you, but to purify you. I have used pain as a tool, not a weapon." Your suffering did not surprise Him. He saw it, He allowed it for a purpose, and He never abandoned you in it. What felt like breaking was actually shaping. What felt like punishment was actually preparation. Refining is the process that removes what is harming you so the true you — the healed, mature, spiritually grounded you — can emerge.

Application:

1. *Understand that the pain you faced had purpose, even when it didn't make sense.*

    Applying this verse starts with accepting that your hardest seasons were not wasted. The heartbreak, the divorce, the financial struggle, the trauma, the isolation, the disappointment — none of it was random. God uses affliction the way a surgeon uses a scalpel: carefully, intentionally, and with healing in mind. When you see your past through this lens, shame loses its power. You begin to recognize how God used pressure to reveal strength, used loss to reveal dependence, and used pain to reveal purpose. This doesn't mean He caused all your suffering, but He certainly used it to shape you into someone wiser, stronger, and more spiritually grounded.

2. *Let your current struggles refine you instead of harden you.*
   Refining exposes hidden things — insecurities, fears, habits, mindsets, and relationships that can't follow you into the next season. In 2025, this might look like God using a stressful job, a difficult relationship, or a season of waiting to show you where you still need healing or where your trust needs to deepen. Instead of becoming bitter or shutting down, open your heart to the question: "Lord, what are You trying to develop or remove in me through this?" Refining hurts, but it transforms you if you surrender to the process instead of resisting it.

3. *Remember that refinement is temporary, but the growth lasts forever.*
   The furnace of affliction is not a permanent home — it is a temporary classroom. Sometimes you feel stuck, like the struggle will never end, but refinement has an expiration date. What God is doing inside you, however, does not. Every season of pressure is producing endurance, wisdom, compassion, humility, and spiritual maturity that will serve you for the rest of your life. When you're in a refining season today, remind yourself that God never leaves you in the fire longer

than necessary. You are coming out different — and better — than you went in.

4. *Use this scripture to shift how you see yourself after hardship.*
    Many people walk through affliction and come out feeling damaged. But this verse teaches the opposite: refinement means you came out more valuable. God didn't destroy you in the fire — He developed you in it. In a society where trauma is often worn as identity, this scripture allows you to say, "I am not what happened to me; I am who God shaped me to be through it." You can walk confidently knowing that God allowed only the heat necessary to grow you, and nothing you went through diminished your worth.

5. *Live with the expectation that refined people get reassigned.*
    God does not refine you and then return you to the same place, same mindset, same relationships, or same cycle. Refinement comes before elevation. If God has refined you, He is preparing you for something. This means you should expect doors to shift, connections to change, opportunities to open, and responsibility to increase. When you accept refinement, you position yourself for divine placement. Let this scripture help you embrace what God is doing — not just in the past, but in your future.

Repeat After Me: If God allowed the fire, it's because I am worth refining — and I will not come out the same.

1 Samuel 16:7 - But the Lord said unto Samuel,
Look not on his countenance, or on the height of his
stature; because I have refused him: for the Lord seeth
not as man seeth; for man looketh on the outward
appearance, but the Lord looketh on the heart.

Meaning:

In this verse, God is correcting Samuel's perspective. Samuel is looking at someone who looks like a king — tall, strong, impressive, polished. But God stops him and says, "Don't choose based on what you can see with your eyes." Humans judge value based on outward things: beauty, status, charisma, talent, confidence, and the image someone presents. But God sees beyond presentation — He sees intention, character, motives, purity, and truth.

This verse reveals that God does not base His choices on outward qualifications. He is drawn to the heart — your honesty, your willingness, your humility, your compassion, and your desire for Him. The world may overlook someone because they don't "look the part," but God looks at who they truly are. He chooses based on qualities that can't be filtered, posed, or faked.

Application:

1. *Stop judging your worth by how you look compared to others.*
   In a world obsessed with appearance, social media aesthetics, body image, and curated identities, it is easy to believe your value comes from external things. But this scripture frees you from that pressure. God is not choosing you, loving you, or using you because of how polished or perfect you appear. He

is drawn to your heart — your sincerity, your desire to grow, and your willingness to follow Him. Even if others overlook you or underestimate you, God sees the parts of you they cannot see. This truth helps you stop chasing external validation and rest in the identity God has already given you.

2. *Allow God to shape your character instead of focusing only on your image.*
   This verse reminds us that character matters far more than presentation. In today's culture, it's easy to build a brand while neglecting the soul, to chase influence before wisdom, or to perfect the outside while avoiding the inner work. But God elevates people whose hearts are aligned with Him. Applying this scripture means prioritizing integrity, honesty, humility, compassion, and spiritual growth over looking impressive. When your heart is right, God can trust you with more — and He can trust you to carry it well.

3. *Be mindful not to judge others based on what you see.*
   We often overlook people who don't look successful, polished, spiritual, or "qualified." But this scripture warns us not to make surface-level assumptions. The person who looks like they have nothing to offer might be carrying an anointing, a calling, or a strength you cannot see. Applying this scripture means asking God for discernment instead of relying on your eyes. When you stop making snap judgments and start seeing people the way God does, you create space for divine connections, unexpected blessings, and relationships that are built on substance instead of image.

4. *Trust that God will open the right doors for you even if you don't "look the part."*

   Many people feel unqualified because they don't fit society's description of success — not thin enough, not educated enough, not wealthy enough, not experienced enough, not pretty enough, not polished enough. But God chooses people who are overlooked, underestimated, and dismissed by others. He chose David — a forgotten shepherd boy — to be king. Applying this verse means believing that God's hand is not limited by your appearance, your background, or your past. If God sees your heart and has chosen you, no rejection, no insecurity, and no human opinion can stop your purpose.

5. *Let this verse heal the parts of you that were judged, rejected, or misunderstood.*

   Many people carry wounds from being judged based on their looks, their weight, their skin color, their past, their mistakes, their social status, or their presentation. This scripture reminds you that God has never judged you that way. He has always seen your heart. He knows your intentions, your growth, your sacrifice, your tears, and the parts of you that no one applauds. Applying this verse means letting God affirm you in places where people misjudged you. It means trusting His vision of you more than their opinions.

Repeat After Me: God sees my heart — not my image. My worth is rooted in His view of me, not the world's.

Proverbs 4:7 - Wisdom is the principal thing; therefore get wisdom: and with all thy getting get understanding.

Meaning:

This scripture is saying that wisdom isn't just important — it's essential. Out of everything you pursue in life, wisdom should come first. Wisdom is not just knowing facts; it's knowing how to live. It's the ability to make good decisions, to discern right from wrong, to recognize danger, and to understand what leads to peace, stability, and spiritual growth.

"Get understanding" means don't just collect information — learn how to apply it. It's possible to know scripture but not understand how to live it. It's possible to hear advice but not grasp the deeper meaning behind it. God wants you to seek wisdom and then seek the understanding that helps you walk it out. In other words, wisdom tells you what is right, and understanding shows you how to do it.

Application:

1. *Seek wisdom before making decisions instead of reacting out of emotion.*

   In today's world, people move quickly — emotionally, financially, relationally, and spiritually. Applying this verse means slowing down long enough to ask, "Is this wise?" before you make a choice. Wisdom helps you avoid unnecessary heartbreak, financial mistakes, toxic relationships, rushed decisions, and spiritual confusion. God gives wisdom through prayer, scripture, wise counsel, and the

Holy Spirit's nudges. When you make wisdom your first priority, your life becomes more stable, less chaotic, and more aligned with God's will.

2. *Ask God to give you understanding so you can apply what you learn.*

   Understanding is what turns scripture into action. It's what helps you say, "Lord, I hear You — now show me how to do this in real life." In 2025, with information coming from everywhere — podcasts, TikTok, sermons, friends, culture — understanding helps you filter out noise and discern what is actually from God. When you seek understanding, you won't just know verses about forgiveness; you'll understand how to forgive. You won't just know you should have boundaries; you'll understand how to build them. Understanding turns knowledge into transformation.

3. *Be intentional about growing mentally, emotionally, and spiritually.*

   Getting wisdom requires effort. It means reading your Bible, studying, reflecting, asking questions, attending church, going to therapy, surrounding yourself with wise voices, and being willing to learn. Wisdom is not passive — it requires pursuit. In a generation where many people rely on feelings or trends, applying this scripture means choosing depth over surface-level thinking and maturity over impulsiveness. The more you grow, the more clearly you will hear God and the better decisions you will make.

4. *Surround yourself with people who carry wisdom, not just opinions.*

   Not everyone is qualified to speak into your life. Applying this scripture means being selective about who you seek advice from. Wisdom may come from someone older, younger, or simply someone who has walked closely with God. Understanding comes when you sit under voices that challenge you to grow, not voices that feed your impulses or your ego. When you surround yourself with wise people, your discernment sharpens and your life aligns more closely with God's purpose.

5. *Let wisdom guide your responses, relationships, and daily choices.*

   Every day offers opportunities to live out this scripture — how you handle conflict, spend money, choose friendships, date, parent your children, nurture your faith, and navigate challenges. Wisdom tells you when to speak up and when to stay quiet, when to move forward and when to pause, when to hold on and when to let go. Understanding helps you see the why behind those decisions. When both are operating in your life, you begin to walk with confidence, clarity, and peace.

Repeat After Me: Wisdom guides my steps, and understanding shows me how to walk them out.

Psalm 51:10 - Create in me a clean heart,
O God; and renew a right spirit within me.

Meaning:

This scripture is David's prayer after he realized how far he'd drifted from God. Instead of pretending he was fine or trying to fix himself, he asked God to create a clean heart in him. The word "create" is important — it means starting fresh, making something new, not just repairing what's broken. David is saying, "God, I can't purify myself. I need You to do the work in me."

When he asks for a "right spirit," he's asking God to restore his inner posture — his attitude, motives, desires, thinking, and spiritual direction. It's a prayer for alignment. A prayer for God to remove what's toxic and restore what's true. It's a recognition that real transformation happens from the inside out, and only God can produce that change.

Application:

1. *Ask God to cleanse what you cannot change on your own.*
   There are some habits, desires, thoughts, and hurts that you can't fix through willpower. Applying this verse means being honest about the parts of your heart that need God's intervention — bitterness, jealousy, lust, anger, pride, unforgiveness, or emotional wounds you've buried. Instead of pretending you're healed or strong, you invite God into the places where you feel weak, ashamed, or stuck. God is not intimidated by what needs cleaning; He specializes in rebuilding hearts that feel damaged or messy.

2. *Be willing to examine your motives and inner posture.*
   A "right spirit" is about what's happening beneath the surface — your intentions, your attitude, the way you respond to correction, the thoughts you entertain, and the way you treat people privately. In 2025, when outward appearance is everything, this verse calls you to do the inner work. Let God show you where your spirit has become tired, irritated, defensive, selfish, fearful, or distracted. True spiritual growth comes when you allow Him to realign you, not just clean you.

3. *Invite God to renew you instead of recycling old patterns.*
   Renewal means becoming refreshed, restored, and redirected. Sometimes life leaves you spiritually drained — worn out from responsibilities, relationships, trauma, stress, or grief. Asking God to "renew a right spirit" means asking Him to revive you where you've gone numb, discouraged, or spiritually dry. Renewal may look like clarity returning to your mind, peace settling in your heart, or desire for God rising again after a long season of silence. God doesn't just clean you; He restores you to who you were meant to be.

4. *Let go of guilt so God can make room for transformation.*
   Many people read this verse and think they have to punish themselves before God will change them. But David's prayer teaches the opposite — transformation starts with surrender, not shame. Applying this verse means releasing the guilt that tells you, "God won't help me because I messed up." God cleans hearts that ask to be cleaned. He renews spirits that admit they need renewal. Your honesty creates space for His healing.

5. *Be intentional about keeping your heart soft and open.*

   Once God begins to clean and renew you, you must guard your heart from slipping back into old places. This means paying attention to influences, environments, conversations, relationships, and habits that contaminate your spirit. In today's world, guarding your heart might look like limiting social media, distancing yourself from toxic people, choosing forgiveness when it's hard, or spending more time in God's presence. A clean heart must be protected, and a renewed spirit must be nurtured.

Repeat After Me: God is not done with my heart — He is cleansing me, renewing me, and shaping me from the inside out.

John 15:13 — Greater love hath no man than this,
that a man lay down his life for his friends.

Meaning:

This scripture is Jesus explaining the highest form of love He would ever demonstrate — giving His life for us. When He speaks of laying down one's life, He is pointing directly to His sacrifice on the cross. But He is also defining what real love looks like: selfless, sacrificial, and willing to give for the good of another.

This verse shows that love is not just emotion; it's action. It costs something. It gives. It protects. It puts others before convenience and comfort. Jesus was teaching that His love is the standard — not the world's version of love that changes based on feelings, mood, or convenience. His love is a commitment backed by sacrifice.

Application:

1. *Recognize that Jesus' sacrifice is the purest form of love you will ever receive.*

   In a world where relationships are often conditional, temporary, or self-serving, this verse grounds you in a love that never changes. Jesus laid down His life not because you earned it, but because He chose you. Applying this verse means allowing His love to redefine your sense of worth and security. You don't have to fight to be loved, beg to be chosen, or perform to be accepted — Jesus already proved your value through the cross. This truth frees you from chasing unhealthy love that drains your spirit.

2. *Let this verse reshape how you love others.*

    Laying down your life doesn't always mean dying for someone; it means living sacrificially. In everyday life, this looks like showing up for people even when it's inconvenient, being patient when you feel frustrated, forgiving when your pride tells you not to, and extending grace when it isn't deserved. Applying this scripture means practicing love that costs something — time, ego, comfort, or effort. Real love isn't passive; it requires a willingness to give of yourself.

3. *Be careful not to confuse sacrificial love with self-destruction.*

    In 2025, many people overextend themselves emotionally, financially, or spiritually and call it "love." But this scripture does not mean letting people abuse you, drain you, or break you. Jesus laid down His life willingly and purposefully — not because He lacked boundaries, but because He loved from a place of strength. Applying this verse means loving others in a healthy, Christ-like way that reflects sacrifice without losing yourself. You can love someone deeply and still protect your mental, emotional, and spiritual well-being.

4. *Use this verse to evaluate the relationships in your life.*

    Healthy relationships involve mutual sacrifice. If you are always giving but never receiving, carrying all the weight, or being treated in ways that contradict God's love, the relationship may need reevaluation. Sacrificial love goes both ways. Applying this scripture means paying attention to who shows up for you, who prays for you, who protects your heart, and who supports your growth. Godly love creates safety, not confusion.

5. *Let Jesus' example become your personal standard for love.*
   This scripture reminds you not to settle for surface-level love — the kind that disappears when things get difficult. When you measure love by Christ's example, you stop accepting relationships that leave you empty and start desiring connections rooted in sacrifice, honor, and mutual care. It also challenges you to love others in a way that reflects Christ: generously, intentionally, and with humility. His love becomes the lens through which you build friendships, date, parent, forgive, and serve.

Repeat After Me: Jesus proved my worth through His sacrifice — and His love is the standard I choose to live by."

ABOUT THE AUTHOR

I am just a woman who's been through it — the storms, the heartbreak, the silent battles, and the sleepless nights. A mother, a friend, a fighter, and a child of God who learned that grace isn't just a word — it's a lifeline. I have survived domestic violence, endured the pain of divorce, faced the challenges of raising children with health issues, experienced gun violence first-hand, and grieved the loss of someone I loved deeply. Through every moment, I discovered this truth: God's love never left me, even when I tried to run from it.

I don't claim perfection. I am still learning. Still healing. Still growing. But I'm committed to telling my story so that someone else out there will know they are not alone. I write with raw honesty, showing up messy but willing, because I believe that's where real transformation begins.

> If you take nothing else from these pages, let it be this:
> **God wants you. Exactly as you are.**
> Broken. Confused. Searching.
> And He's not finished with you yet.
> This is just the beginning.

NEED MORE SUPPORT? DIVE DEEPER WITH THIS BONUS TOOL

God isn't finished with your story. Whether you're reading this book alone or in a group, I created a tool to help you keep walking forward, one page at a time.

The Full Devotional Workbook

Want more space, more guidance, and printable worksheets? Grab the full version which includes extra scripture studies, "My Breakthrough Moment" journal pages, prayer logs, and deeper prompts.

Visit: www.RenewedInk.com

www.ingramcontent.com/pod-product-compliance
Lightning Source LLC
Chambersburg PA
CBHW060420130626
46555CB00005B/2150